T0065173

RAISING AN
AUTISTIC
YOUNG ADULT

A Parents' Guide to ASD Safety,
Communication, and Employment Opportunities to Empower
Black and Brown Caregivers and Their Families

ESTHER DILLARD

ARCHWAY
PUBLISHING

Archway Publishing books may be ordered through booksellers or by contacting:

Archway Publishing
1663 Liberty Drive
Bloomington, IN 47403
www.archwaypublishing.com
844-669-3957

Because of the dynamic nature of the Internet, any web addresses or links contained in this book may have changed since publication and may no longer be valid. The views expressed in this work are solely those of the author and do not necessarily reflect the views of the publisher, and the publisher hereby disclaims any responsibility for them.

Any people depicted in stock imagery provided by Getty Images are models, and such images are being used for illustrative purposes only. Certain stock imagery © Getty Images.

Content warning: Chapter 6 contains true stories about violence against teens and adults with autism.

ISBN: 978-1-6657-5251-0 (sc)
ISBN: 978-1-6657-5252-7 (e)

Library of Congress Control Number: 2023921002

Print information available on the last page.

Archway Publishing rev. date: 12/26/2023

CONTENTS

Introduction ix

Chapter 1 Understanding the Spectrum 1

Taking a Look at the Spectrum 3

Looking Under the ASD Umbrella 3

Autistic Disorder (Classic Autism) 3

Asperger's Syndrome 4

Pervasive Developmental Disorder-Not Otherwise Specified (PDD-NOS) 4

Childhood Disintegrative Disorder (CDD) 4

High-Functioning Autism (HFA) 4

Verbal vs. Nonverbal Autism 5

Nick's First Real Conversation 5

Autism Across the Ages 6

Young Children/Toddlers 6

Tweens and Teenagers 8

Diagnosis Discussion with Dr. Franklin 9

Common Myths About Autism 12

Autism Is Caused By… 12

Only Children Have Autism 13

Autism Is a Disease and Can Be Cured 13

People With ASD Have Intellectual Challenges and/
or Savant Syndrome 14

People With Autism Are Unemotional, Aggressive,
or Anti-social 14

Dr. Spinks-Franklin on Aggressive Behaviors 15

Chapter 2 Common Challenges 18

  Adolescence and the Autistic Child 18

      Sensory Issues 21

      Emotional Self-regulation 22

         Depression 23

         Anger and Meltdowns.. 23

         Overwhelm 24

         Anxiety 24

      Jeremiah and the Rain 26

      Transitions 27

      Special Interests 28

  Anger Management with Darryl and Jabaar 29

      Bullying..31

      Mental Health 33

Chapter 3 Day-to-day Dilemmas 35

  Avery's Haircut 35

  Executive Functioning.. 38

      Tips on How to Improve Your Teen's Executive

      Functioning 40

  Organization with Rachel Williams 41

  Helping Your Teen Manage and Understand Themselves........ 44

      Personal Hygiene 44

      Stimming 46

      Keeping Their Spaces in Order 47

      Transportation 48

      Beyond Graduation 49

Chapter 4 The Social Teen.................................... 51

  Social Cues with Dr. Durr..51

  Autism and Social Challenges 52

  Improving Your Teen's Social Skills.................................53

  Helping Your Teen With Relationships............................ 56

  Having "The Sex Talk" With Nick 58

  Sex and Relationships 60

Chapter 5 Learning and Growing 63
Autism and Education with Dr. Hannon 63
Helping Your Teen Through School 64
The Power of Labels 67
Academic Challenges for Black and Brown Teens 68
Attending School with Dr. Durr 70
Helping Your Teen Practice Self-Care 72
    Medication 74
    Teen Care and Therapy 76
Teen Care with Janet Jones-Jordan 78

Chapter 6 Staying Safe 80
The Safety Talk 80
Teaching Your Child How to Be Safe 83
    Developing a Safety Plan 84
    Teaching Self-Advocacy Skills 84
    Teaching Stranger Safety 85
    Teaching Technology Safety 85
    Teaching Emergency Procedures 86
Autism and the Police With Dr. Onaiwu and Ms. Proctor 86
Safety for Teens with Dr. Durr 91
Autism and the Road Ahead 93

Chapter 7 Employment and Resources 95
Job-Hunting with ASD 95
Employment Opportunities 98
Resources 100
    Autism Society 100
    Resources for Families 100
    Grants and Scholarships 100
    National Autism Association 100
    Resources for Parents 100
    Helping Hand Program 101
    Interactive Autism Network 101
    Parent Resources 101

Autism Parenting Magazine 101
    Parenting Resources 101
Family Voices...101
    Autism Resources 101
    Financial Resources..102
Parent to Parent USA 102
    State Chapters...102
National Parent Helpline...102
    Autism and Special Needs Support 102
    Apps to Try Out..103

Conclusion...105
References..107

INTRODUCTION

I honestly thought, before I took a step toward parenthood, that I had it figured out. You see, I grew up in a household full of kids. My father was a Christian minister who worked another job during the week for the New York State Health Department, and my mother was a foster mom who stayed home. She had kidney issues, which eventually led to 12 years on dialysis, so I was the "go-to" in the house when it came to many mommy duties. For years I shared one main bathroom with 8-10 girls at a time. My parents often had 4-6 foster children in our home at a time, and a few cousins and church family members shared our home throughout the years as well. I was the oldest child, so I often had to be the person who helped Mom coordinate showers and do the laundry, as well as cook and distribute meals at home.

I learned quickly how to shop and cook on a budget for a family of 10. I learned to change diapers and make a coordinated schedule of bottle feedings from formula by the time I was around 9 years old. I helped with potty training, walking, feeding, and teaching kids how to read. And by the time I became a teenager, I did not want any kids— at least not early. I wanted to pursue a career first and get married. I wanted the traditional route. So when I saw others who had children, single or married, I figured, "been there, done that, I can handle it. I just want it on my own terms." But I learned quickly when I started my own motherhood journey that sometimes when that little bundle of joy arrives, you get handed something you didn't expect. That is what happened to me.

When Nicholas arrived in my life in 2008, I noticed that my treasure was just a little bit different. Just months before this, I had left a job as an anchor and reporter for WEYI in Flint, Michigan. We had recently moved twice since we first learned I got pregnant, once to Washington, DC where my husband took a program directing job at WPGC 95.5 FM. After only six months, he was offered a job as a program director for WBLS in New York. I had no full-time steady job. My husband was the sole paycheck. And I was in a position I hadn't been in before. I was a "stay-at-home mom" who was working part-time at jobs I picked up that didn't pay much. I was happy to have a child because we had tried for seven years to get pregnant. But learning about autism was a completely different journey. I had no idea what it was or how to "fix it." The only reference I had was the movie *Rain Man*. All my life I had learned how to "fix things" when faced with challenges. There was no fix for this.

I had to get over the grief of not having a child who completed his milestones as it said in many baby books. I spent many years reading and sharing with others about the experiences of the Special Needs community. I hope that in sharing my story, and those of others, I will be able to inspire you and provide you with strategies you can use today. This book also offers added perspectives from Black and Latino parents and autistic adults who have experienced many challenges. Many of the interviews I share in this book are from my recent years working as an anchor and reporter for the Black Information Network, 0wned by iHeartMedia. I was in a position that aided me in interviewing experts, autistic adults, and parents of autistic teens to learn more about autism.

Statistics show that, over the next ten years, approximately seven thousand to 1.1 million teens will enter adulthood and lose access to many autism services offered by schools. When compared with other special healthcare needs, it was shown that teens with autism are half as likely to receive healthcare transition services, especially when they have other medical conditions associated with autism. Access to healthcare becomes a lot more limited once they no longer see a pediatrician (Laxman et al., 2019).

These statistics mean that we need to get more proactive about supporting people with autism and autistic families—this is a serious social problem. People of color in disadvantaged communities faced with these challenges need extra understanding and support. After learning about the experiences of the autistic community, I became motivated to create a platform to help give voice to those who have remained unheard and to reach out and help parents of children with autism. I was touched to hear so many experiences that mirrored my own as a parent and to learn so much that I did not know.

I remember clearly the feelings of grief and loss that I experienced after receiving my son's diagnosis. It felt as if many of the expectations that I had for my son's future would remain unrealized, and I mourned the loss of the "typical" childhood I had envisioned for him. Many of my interviews involved conversations about the struggle with feelings of disappointment and sadness.

As parents of children with autism, we worry about our children's futures and feel overwhelmed by the responsibilities of caregiving. The truth is, caring for a child with autism can be stressful and anxiety-provoking, particularly if the child has challenging behaviors or co-occurring conditions such as anxiety or ADHD. Sensory overload, changes in routine, difficulty communicating needs, and many other things may lead to meltdowns, aggression, and self-injury. We are human, and sometimes we cannot help but feel overwhelmed, frustrated, and helpless when trying to cope with these behaviors.

Raising an autistic child can be isolating, as we sometimes find it challenging to connect with other parents or to participate in social activities that other families take for granted. Several of the Black and Brown parents that I spoke with shared that they sometimes do not feel comfortable or welcome in some established groups that have predominantly Caucasian members because leadership sometimes does not factor in culture or ethnicity in their approach.

It is often so challenging to find appropriate services to support our children. Specialized care and services such as speech and occupational therapy, applied behavior analysis (ABA), and social skills training are not always easy to access, especially in areas where there are limited resources or long waiting lists. Our finances are also affected. The cost of therapy, medications, and specialized education can also add up quickly, and some parents find that they need to reduce their work hours or leave their jobs altogether to provide full-time care for their children.

Our children are wonderful, unique individuals, but sometimes it is a struggle to get others to see this side of them. Despite increasing awareness and understanding of autism, many people still hold negative stereotypes and misconceptions about the condition. The devastating reality is that we often find ourselves and our children facing stigma and discrimination. Some cultural groups even stand steadfast in denial against autism and how it affects our children's behavior.

Faced with all this, we cannot help but wish for understanding and acceptance for our children and our families. It is painful when others dismiss our problems and say our children are just "naughty" or when they use the "r-word." As parents, we want our children to succeed; enjoy life, manage themselves daily, and live comfortably and happily.

When the roadmap to my journey with my son shifted, I decided that I would not just make a change, but I would do my best to be a change. In writing this book, I have worked to ensure that I can provide some information from experts along with some viewpoints from autistic adults and parents who have navigated this time with their growing autistic teen.

I wanted to choose voices that are not often highlighted in many articles and texts. For this reason, this book gives voice to African American and Latino voices who add perspective to the intersectionality of both of those worlds and the worlds of autism, culture, and ethnicity. Although the general definitions and scientific explanations apply to anyone on the Spectrum, I chose to interview those in the Black and Brown community to share their unique experiences living their ASD reality. By sharing what I have learned and experienced, I hope to address some of the questions a parent may have when facing a new chapter in their child's development—adolescence.

***

Note: All interview participants have given me their permission to use their words in this book.

CHAPTER 1

UNDERSTANDING THE SPECTRUM

Autism is part of my child. It's not everything he is.
My child is so much more than a diagnosis.
–S.L. Westendorf-Coelho

When my son was first diagnosed with autism, it was a day filled with emotion. I was in the doctor's office, and I was anxious because I wanted the doctor to confirm everything I had read and studied on the subject of autism. Nick had missed a few milestones. He often did not make eye contact. He loved to spin in circles, and he never really spoke to me; he only repeated phrases.

Despite this, I spent hours teaching Nicholas how to read by playing with flashcards and soft plush letters I sewed by hand. I felt that if he could repeat words, perhaps he could recognize symbols with pictures and make the association. I had always learned from my parents to "work with what you got." It's a simple rule of thumb that helped me for years in my personal life and career. And even though my mom was no longer physically here on earth at the time, I used this as a first-time parent.

My father bought me the video series *Your Baby Can Read* by Dr. Robert Titzer. And even though Nick was only about three and a half when I made an appointment with a developmental pediatrician, he had zipped through the videos and flash cards provided in a flash.

One day I caught him repeating an entire skit from Sesame Street word for word. I was shocked. My kid is smart. I know he is. I just can't seem to get him to talk TO ME rather than AT ME.

The doctor sat in a small chair while Nicholas played with toys on the floor. He was in heaven. He had toy cars and blocks of all kinds. He barely looked at the lady who asked him questions and then played with him on the floor. I remember she asked me plenty of questions.

After about 20 minutes, she said, "Your son is echolalic." I had never heard the term until then.

"What's that?" I asked.

She explained it's when a child repeats the words you say to them rather than responding. At the end of a long explanation of a lot of different things, she said Nick had autism.

I knew it. I just wanted her to say it. I wanted her to put it on paper and make it official. I knew that even though this diagnosis was scary, I could use what I got. God dealt me this hand—so let's roll up our sleeves and work with it. Use it as a tool to get my child the additional support he needs to move forward toward a better future. It was scary. Later at home, I cried in my room with the door closed. Would he ever talk to me? I was worried about people in our lives who might try to keep him from achieving his potential because of a label. In fact, I remember distinctly, my husband's parents did NOT want me to get a diagnosis. They felt as a parent of a Black boy, this was going to limit my son's future. This is not uncommon for many Black parents I have spoken to on this subject. And I get it.

There have been studies that show in the past that Black boys were thrown into special education because of educators who are quick to do this because of what they label as behavioral problems.

McNair (2021) published an article noting that Black males in grades 3 to 8 are often incorrectly assigned to special education, but other supports could better help them succeed in school. My husband's parents just didn't want their grandson labeled. They believed that label would limit his future opportunities and access to higher education. However, I didn't see the label as a limit but as a starting point for me to determine what I may need to overcome, and from the defined language of diagnosis determine a way of working around those "perceived limitations." However, I want you to know that just because there is a diagnosis does not mean that everything associated with the label has to be true for your child. And if it is, it doesn't mean that the characteristics or development of your child can't change. I encourage you to "use what you got." You may be surprised by what happens.

TAKING A LOOK AT THE SPECTRUM

Autism Spectrum Disorder (ASD) is present from birth and is characterized by differences in brain development that affects how individuals communicate, socialize, and behave (Nightengale, 2021). People with autism view and experience the world differently, and this influences their thoughts, emotions, and actions. Symptoms include restricted and repetitive behavioral patterns and difficulty with social interactions. In the past, it was thought to be a single disorder. However, it is now seen as being on a "spectrum" as everyone experiences different symptoms to varying degrees from mild to severe. The acknowledgment that each person's experience with autism is unique helps to reduce stigma and promote understanding of ASD. It has now been recognized that those diagnosed with other disorders—for example, Asperger's syndrome—are also on the autism spectrum.

Looking Under the ASD Umbrella

Autistic Disorder (Classic Autism)

This is the most severe form of autism and is characterized by significant social, communication, and behavioral challenges. People with this disorder may have delayed language development, difficulty in making eye contact, repetitive behaviors, and intense interest in specific topics. Some people characterize people with this as needing "high support." I prefer this definition rather than "low-functioning." I will explain why in a moment.

Asperger's Syndrome

This is a milder form of autism that affects social interaction and communication. People with this disorder often have above-average intelligence, but may have difficulty understanding social cues and may struggle with repetitive behaviors. I prefer to use the definition of "low support" rather than "high functioning." I think Color of Autism Foundation founder Camille Proctor put it best when she told me in an interview with the Black Information Network that "it doesn't matter if you are the smartest person in the room and you can't relate to anyone or you have no friends." Support is still needed, just at different levels. It doesn't make one superior over the other. It just may make it easier for a parent to function in their everyday lives.

Pervasive Developmental Disorder-Not Otherwise Specified (PDD-NOS)

Also known as atypical autism, this is characterized by mild to moderate impairments in social interaction and communication. People with PDD-NOS may have fewer and less severe symptoms than those with autistic disorder or Asperger's syndrome.

Childhood Disintegrative Disorder (CDD)

CDD is a rare disorder that affects language, social, and motor skills. Children with CDD develop normally until the age of 2-4 years and then experience a significant and irreversible loss of previously acquired skills.

High-Functioning Autism (HFA)

This term is used to describe individuals with autism spectrum disorder (ASD) who have average or above-average intellectual abilities and good verbal skills. People with HFA often have difficulty with social communication, repetitive behaviors, and sensory processing. The term "high-functioning" is controversial because it implies that individuals with HFA have an advantage over those with lower-functioning autism. However, this is not necessarily true, as people with HFA can still face significant challenges in daily life, such as difficulty with social interactions and sensory overload

Verbal vs. Nonverbal Autism

Verbal autism, also known as high-functioning autism, refers to individuals with ASD who have good verbal communication skills and can speak and understand language fluently. However, they may still face challenges in social interactions, such as difficulty understanding nonverbal cues, social reciprocity, and social imagination.

In my interviews with experts, nonverbal autism has also been referred to as nonspeaking autism. This is because individuals with limited or no verbal communication skills may still be able to communicate, just not with audible words using their vocal chords. These individuals may communicate through nonverbal means, such as gestures, facial expressions, or pointing. They may also use assistive communication devices or technology.

It's important to note that there is a wide range of communication abilities within the autism spectrum, and some individuals may have a combination of verbal and nonverbal communication skills.

NICK'S FIRST REAL CONVERSATION

For a little more than three and a half years, Nicholas only repeated. He was really good at it, too. But instead of getting frustrated, I made it a game. When I said, "Good morning, Nicholas!" he'd repeat "Good Morning, Nicholas!" with the very same tone. I would then follow up with "Good Morning, Mom, how are you?" which he also repeated.

I started to do it with everything. I'd say, "How are you doing, baby?" He'd say, "How are you doing, baby?" I'd then say what I wanted him to say: "Oh, I'm doing good, Mom." This of course did get a little exasperating at times, but I believed if I kept my mind open and did it playfully with love, he wouldn't pick up on my frustration but instead feel the love I had for whatever way he responded. Nick, I learned, picked up on my mood very quickly. If I was angry, sad, or frustrated, he would come over and hug me and stroke my face. The nonverbal emotion in the room was easy for him to spot.

I will never forget the first time he initiated a change in our daily conversational routine. I said "I love you, Nicholas," and my darling boy responded "I love you, Mom," while still looking at his toy. I froze. Then I hugged the stuffing out of him with tears in my eyes. It was the day I knew he was going to talk TO ME, not AT ME. Now as a teenager, my son is an incessant talker who wants to engage me and anyone else in conversation.

AUTISM ACROSS THE AGES

Symptoms of autism may present differently depending on the age of the individual. These symptoms are usually noticeable by around year 2 of a child's life. Your child may not present all of the symptoms I am about to mention, and the severity of each symptom will vary.

Young Children/Toddlers

Young children with autism may show inconsistencies in certain communicative behaviors.

- They do not always respond to their names when called.
- Gestures such as waving, smiling, and nodding are rarely initiated or returned unless someone asks them to do it.
- They rarely make eye contact with you, even when they want or are excited about something. Similarly, lifting and pointing at things does not happen often.

- Simple one-step instructions such as "sit on the chair" or "give me the doll" are difficult for them to follow.
- They rarely babble and, if they do, it does not appear as if they are doing so in an effort to communicate with you.
- They rarely mimic the actions and behaviors of the people they see in their environment. For example, they will not return your kisses or pretend to do the things they see you doing (washing dishes, talking on the phone, and so on).

Some toddlers and young children with ASD may show fixed and/or repetitive behaviors.

- They show preference to their toys and possessions being in a specific order and get upset when this order is disturbed. Children may spend a long time lining up their toys, and do so each time they play with them. When interacting with these toys, they consistently do so in the same way, and rarely engage in pretend play.
- They show strong, obsessive interests in things, or focus intently on parts of an object.
- Once an interest in an activity has been formed, they get upset if prevented from engaging in that activity.
- They develop specific routines that they have to follow, or move their bodies repeatedly in certain ways: for example, flapping their hands or spinning in circles.
- They repeat words and phrases over and over.

Some children will avoid physical contact and may show extreme sensitivity to sensory input (sights, sounds, smells, tastes, textures/touch). While some may shy away from strong sensations, others may constantly seek them out. Other symptoms of ASD that may be presented are delayed language, movement and learning skills, and irregular eating and sleeping habits. Children may either lack fear or be excessively fearful and display anxiety and stress. They may be impulsive or hyperactive, or struggle to focus. Some children may even have seizures.

Tweens and Teenagers

Navigating social situations can be challenging for older children and teenagers with autism.

- They have difficulty waiting their turns in conversations. It is easy for them to chatter away a mile a minute, while at the same time refraining from speaking much about themselves. While they can talk at length about things they are interested in, it becomes difficult for them once the topic veers to something they do not care about.
- Showing empathy is hard, as they are not very good at reading the emotions of others or picking up on the general mood of a group of people. I would like to note that this is not a rule. Some children, like my own, appear to pick up emotions with people very easily but are unsure how to handle it.
- Common phrases can be difficult for them to understand as they take things literally. A tween or teenager with ASD may be quite confused if told to "break a leg."
- When speaking, they use a monotone or slightly louder voice, accompanied by very few, if any, gestures. They also rarely make eye contact or change their expressions in a way that allows others to tell what they are feeling or thinking. They are also very formal and precise in their speech.
- They completely miss social cues or misunderstand gestures. Adapting to different social situations is difficult, as they do not know how to adjust their behaviors to match their environment. They also may not understand social rules or personal space.
- Making and keeping friendships can be very difficult for them, and they may prefer to spend their time alone.

Tweens and teens may also display fixed and repetitive behaviors.

- They develop strict routines or rules for play that everyone has to follow, and any violation of these rules or inability to complete a routine can lead to the teen getting upset.
- Certain actions and behaviors become repetitive or seem compulsive. They may develop fixed interests in certain activities and spend a majority of their time engaging in them.
- Toys or objects may gain particular significance to them, and they may carry these around with them as much as possible.

Tweens and teenagers may also struggle to cope with school. They may experience anxiety, depression, and trouble with eating and sleeping. Sensory input can cause very strong reactions, and they either try to avoid things that affect their senses or seek out strong sensations. Some may even display aggressive behavior and/or show less of a reaction to pain than other children.

It's important to note that the symptoms mentioned for all the ages can be present in other developmental disorders as well, and a formal diagnosis of autism can only be made by a healthcare professional. If you suspect that your child may have autism, seek an evaluation from a pediatrician or a specialist in autism diagnosis and treatment.

DIAGNOSIS DISCUSSION WITH DR. FRANKLIN

Although statistics show that more children are being diagnosed with autism because of increased screenings, many parents I spoke with complain that getting that initial diagnosis is often not easy.

In my audio series *Black, Autistic and Safe*, African American Dr. Adiaha Spinks-Franklin told me during her interview that disparities in diagnosis and access to care still continue. The Board Certified Developmental-Behavioral Pediatrician says her research on this is extensive.

I asked Dr. Franklin her thoughts on why there's such a disparity when it comes to diagnosis for Black and Brown children. She said:

> The short answer is racism. The long answer is multifactorial. For one, when it comes to media and marketing campaigns to increase public awareness of the diagnosis of autism, those campaigns do not usually center the voices of Black, Indigenous, and other people of color—Brown. They're often sent to the voices of suburban middle-class affluent white folks, which is not the majority of people in the country. So when you look at studies, there's actually less information about developments with disabilities, behavior disorders, and mental health conditions in Black, Indigenous, and Brown communities, period. So that's one of the issues. If you don't see it, you don't know you can have it or be it, right?

Dr. Franklin added that the behaviors noted as possible symptoms of autism may vary depending on the cultural experiences and perspectives of the child and their caregivers. These cultural perspectives influence how parents interpret their child's behaviors, affecting how they discuss their concerns with medical personnel.

Talking with Dr. Franklin about culture and autism reminded me of a conversation I once heard. In a hospital, a white nurse came out to express concern about a patient in a hospital bed. She told one of the other nurses that she thought the patient needed psychological services. The Black nurse said, "Okay, what was wrong?" The white nurse said, "She keeps talking and tapping her head while answering questions."

The Black nurse looked a bit confused and went to talk to the patient. When she looked in, she noticed it was a Black woman who was wearing a hair weave. She asked her how she was doing and during the conversation, the patient tapped her head while talking. The Black nurse completed the conversation and then left. She told the white nurse not to write the patient up for any psychological evaluation.

Why? The weave was itching and Black women who have them often tap their head to stop the itching rather than scratching it. She wasn't crazy, she just had an itch. Scratching the weave would dislodge the work a stylist did on her hair. A white woman who doesn't understand this phenomenon in Black hair care would not understand what was happening. They would think there was a problem when there was none.

In our interview, Dr. Franklin also noted that medical providers are overwhelmingly white.

> Only 5% of physicians are Black, only about 7-8 percent are Latino, or Latin-X, about 20% are East and South Asian. The rest are white. And so what we have found in the literature and research is that white physicians are actually less likely to ask Black parents specifically about their concerns about their child's development and behavior. Even when it is abundantly clear the child is at risk or high risk for developmental disability, the white physician might do a screening looking for developmental delays in the child, but they are much less likely to take Black parents' concerns seriously.

Dr. Franklin says statistically, white physicians are less likely to do an appropriate evaluation to get a proper diagnosis.

> So Black kids are more likely to be diagnosed with things like ADHD, intellectual disability, which is the new term for mental retardation. You know they're more likely to be given that diagnosis and then way later, finally get the diagnosis of autism.

She added that delayed diagnosis for Black children puts the child and parents at a disadvantage.

Your window of opportunity for giving your child the services and interventions they need to maximize their development is in those first three or four years. The average Black kid isn't diagnosed with autism until they're like six, seven [years old]. So now we've missed this very important window of opportunity for interventions to be the most effective. It doesn't mean that a child can't get effective interventions at six, seven, eight, and nine. It just means that your brain develops most rapidly in those first three to five years of life. That's when we need to be intervening to make sure your learning, social, and communication skills are maximized so you can function to the best of your ability. [It also allows] your parents [a better chance to have] the resources they need to parent you in the way that you as an autistic person need to be parented and need to be loved and communicated.

Delayed diagnosis can often lead to delayed treatment. And ultimately children growing up without the tools to manage anxiety and sensory sensitivity.

COMMON MYTHS ABOUT AUTISM

While there is more awareness and a drive toward understanding and accepting ASD, many teens unfortunately face prejudice and stigma from those around them. Some of this may be unintentional, but it can lead to assumptions and misunderstandings.

Autism Is Caused By...

Many people insist that autism is caused by childhood trauma, poor diet, infections, bad parenting, or vaccines.

For years, many people have insisted that autism occurs as a result of vaccines given at birth and during childhood. This myth came about as a result of an unscientific research conducted in the 1990s, and the researcher actually later lost his medical license. Similarly, bad parenting being the cause of autism began with the Refrigerator Mother Hypothesis in the 1950s. According to this hypothesis, a child will be traumatized into autism if their mother is emotionally distant or neglectful. (One Central Health, 2020).

In truth, scientists are still working to understand the underlying causes for autism. They believe that disruption in a child's neurodevelopment occurs as a result of a combination of multiple factors. Some people have genetic conditions that may be linked to their autism.

Only Children Have Autism

I mentioned before that autism is present at birth. ASD is a condition that stays throughout an individual's life. It is possible to manage symptoms, but it is not something that one can "just grow out of." ASD in children is often easier to identify than in adults, as challenges with communication are more evident in younger autistic individuals. Research and diagnosis was also primarily focused on autism in children, and have only recently begun to study ASD in adults.

Some people do not receive an ASD diagnosis until they become adults. Symptoms are more noticeable and prevalent during childhood, and often become less so as individuals enter their teenage years and adulthood. As a result, ASD becomes harder to identify as children grow.

Autism Is a Disease and Can Be Cured

This belief is one that has proven harmful to some individuals, as they or their parents may try various unconventional methods in an effort to cure ASD. Some individuals think that autism is a disease and, as such, can be cured. There are those who think that "everyone has autism now" and view it as a condition that is occurring more frequently.

However, as a neurodevelopmental disorder, autism cannot be trained or medicated into nonexistence. Rather than there being a rise in children being born with ASD, there is a rise in understanding the condition. As a result, symptoms become easier to recognize and diagnose.

People With ASD Have Intellectual Challenges and/or Savant Syndrome

Some people apply blanket symptoms to autistic individuals and assume that everyone has intellectual and learning challenges and/or special talents. There are people who believe that having autism means you cannot speak or learn new skills.

Autism is different for each person, which is why it exists on a spectrum. Some individuals do struggle with intellectual challenges and need extra help in the form of proper support and resources to learn and develop their skills. However, this does not apply to every person with ASD. Similarly, savant syndrome really does exist—where some people show extraordinary physical and mental talents—but is seen in only about 10% of autistic individuals (Lovering, 2022).

People With Autism Are Unemotional, Aggressive, or Anti-social

A common symptom of autism is difficulty expressing yourself verbally and nonverbally. This can be interpreted as not being able to feel emotions. However, people with autism do experience the wide range of emotions; some just rarely show it. Problems with social interactions can also lead to people with autism being viewed as anti-social when this is really not the case.

Where violence is concerned, difficulty processing their environment and/or controlling their emotions can lead to autistic children having outbursts. However, they can be taught how to understand and channel what they are feeling. The truth is, children with autism are not more predisposed to violence than others, they just need extra help in managing their emotions and coping with their environments.

DR. SPINKS-FRANKLIN ON AGGRESSIVE BEHAVIORS

I asked Dr. Adiaha Spinks-Franklin what advice she had for parents who are concerned about aggressive behaviors and how to handle them.

> Safety plans are really important. Sometimes when you have an autistic adolescent, an autistic young adult, or an autistic child who has aggressive outbursts, they can be predicted. You know what the triggers are and as a family, a lot of times you know how to avoid the triggers.
>
> Sometimes the outbursts can be completely unpredictable and random, and you just don't know how to prepare for it. But safety is really important. We talk about so many different ways that aggressive behaviors can be addressed and it's not easy, and you got to have a whole toolbox of ideas of how to manage it.

Dr. Franklin noted that she has sometimes given emergency medications to some families who have concerns about their children's aggressive behaviors. These medications can be given orally, dissolve quickly, and help to calm down agitation.

> Parents can consider having a 'safe room' in the house. Let us talk about the child's bedroom for example;

you can reverse the door knob so that the lock to the room is on in the hallway where you can get in and out of the room easily [but the child is not able to do so]. You don't want furniture in the room that the child could pull down on themselves...like a TV they can pull off the wall.

Some families actually buy padding like the gym pads for the walls so that if the child begins to bang their heads, they're not going to injure themselves terribly. If the child needs to throw something, put objects in the room that they're not going to injure themselves when they throw them like cushion blocks. You can give them sponge blocks so they can throw them, and they can have their outburst and their tantrum, but they're not going to break anything and they're not going to injure themselves or knock holes in the wall and things of that sort.

She suggested that if you own the home and don't want to reverse the locks because the child hates being trapped in the room–which is common– then cut the door in half.

So that can be opened and you can see in and out and they can see out, but they can't get out of the room. They can't climb over the door to get out, but at least you have this top half of the door that if you need to close and lock it, you can. You can open it if you can, but your loved one is not able to climb out of the room if it's a safe space.

She added that you should have a village.

Who can you call in an emergency, when your child is having a meltdown that can come and is a good person to help calm down the situation and redirect [your child]? If you have to call law enforcement, specifically ask for crisis intervention and the mental health unit. Tell them 'My child has autism. My child is having a tantrum, we need help'. Be very clear about what you're calling about, so they're not coming in like they are after a criminal.

Dr. Spinks-Franklin added that she talks to all of her parents at her practice about having a clear safety plan worked out ahead of time.

CHAPTER 2

COMMON CHALLENGES

*Don't think that there's a different, better child "hiding"
behind the autism. This is your child. Love the child in front
of you. Encourage his strengths, celebrate his quirks, and
improve his weaknesses, the way you would with any child.*
–C. Scovell LaZebnik

ADOLESCENCE AND THE AUTISTIC CHILD

When my son started his path to adolescence, it was a bumpy ride. He couldn't seem to get along with children who didn't want to be his friend. He wanted to "make them" like him and couldn't understand why one or two children didn't want to include him in conversations or in their circle. It was rough. And I learned this was not atypical for some children on the spectrum. And sometimes, at least in my son's case, the "discussions" or arguments with teachers and counselors and with us at home would go on for long periods of time. Nicholas wanted to argue it in his favor. He also had a difficult time sharing the spotlight and allowing other kids to participate in the process of learning. One woman who helped him through his tweens and early teens was a school counselor named Rachel Williams.

Williams is an African American social worker who has worked with the Ridgefield New Jersey Public school system for 27 years.

The school system has a special program that helps children with a wide range of special needs, including autism. There, the autism program will provide support for your child from kindergarten through high school and even up to 21. Counselors there say they will help some children apply for college or work programs to help them transition into adulthood.

Williams said that in her years of experience, she has seen that it's often difficult for children on the spectrum experiencing adolescence.

> They're dealing with other factors that, you know, the typical kid doesn't necessarily have to deal with. Everything seems a little more heightened when you're dealing with someone on the spectrum. Their emotions are more heightened. They're, you know, maybe more sensitive. It may be difficult for them to verbalize feelings but yet at the same time, a lot of them are very typical, dealing with things that typical teenagers go through. So it's twofold for them. You know, they're dealing with things that are related to their disability.
>
> Also, they're dealing with just being a child and going through the adolescent development, the childhood development period. So it is definitely challenging. I counsel students who are classified, but not necessarily on the spectrum, maybe they have learning disabilities or other issues going on other than autism. So my experience is sort of varied.

She mentioned she definitely found that teens struggle with sensory issues as well.

And in fact, I think their issues are often heightened due to puberty because now we're introducing puberty into the mix and that's a rather tumultuous time in their lives. So I do a lot of work with helping them to find strategies to control their anger.

Williams said she's helped students learn deep breathing techniques and often takes them on cool-down walks to keep a situation from becoming out of control.

We actually have a sensory room at our school, and a lot of times the teachers or myself will take the child to the sensory room where they can have other distractions, so to speak, to help channel some of their anger or feelings. Emotions, you know, to calm them down. I did use fidgets for a while, especially when it first came out. That was really huge. And then our school was like, OK, this is a distraction. So it's like, you know, we use it at a minimum with certain kids.

And we'll tell the teacher, you know, I might say, hey, listen, I gave this to this child. It could be a squishy ball. Squishy animals are really popular with the kids, and I'll say, 'Put it in your pocket and we'll work it out with the teacher, where you could take it out when you're having difficulty regulating your emotions'. They'll keep it in their desk and the teacher will understand, you know, as long as they use it discreetly.

As they become teenagers, they become more aware of their social surroundings and more conscious of what their peers think about them. And that's a big difference where when they're little, they could care less with their peers.

But when they're older, it's about being cool, you know, and their peers might check them and say, like, 'Hey, look, why are you screaming? Why are you crying?' [The kids here are] in high school and that actually is a helpful strategy because, like, you know, you and I as adults could tell them until we're blue in the face: 'Hey, look, this is inappropriate, you have to behave a certain way now that you're in high school, or in this environment.' Their peers will really bring it to light, like, 'Hey, this isn't cool', and I find that the teenagers listen more to their peers a lot of times than the adults. So that's the stage where peers become very important in their lives and have a strong influence on their behaviors.

Sensory Issues

It is very common for people with ASD to also have sensory processing disorder. Some may be extremely sensitive to sensations (hypersensitivity), others are less responsive to sensory stimulations (hyposensitivity), and some experience a mixture of both. For those who are hypersensitive, sights, sounds, tastes, textures, and smells in the world can be very overwhelming and can lead to outbursts, social isolation, a need for structure and routine, and trouble communicating. School, work, and social events can be challenging as they struggle to filter out the noise from others and focus on tasks. When faced with so many sensations, the natural response is avoidance. Those who are hypersensitive dislike being touched, cover their ears when around loud noises, and close their eyes to avoid bright lights.

While people with hypersensitivity try to pull away from strong sensations, individuals who are hyposensitive seek them out. In addition to being attracted to strong smells, sights, tastes, sounds, and interesting textures, they often have difficulty recognizing when they are in pain, hungry, or hot or cold, or when they need to use the bathroom. People with hyposensitivity may make sounds, rock back and forth, and touch things in an effort to make their environment more stimulating.

Individuals with sensory challenges may often violate personal space, chew on items that are not food, and have poor depth perception. They are super sensitive to any changes in their environment, and are clumsy and lack coordination. Other symptoms include talking loudly and quickly, being constantly on the move, and being rough during play. They constantly touch things, and struggle to do two sensory tasks at the same time.

Sensory processing difficulties are common in teens with autism, and can impact their ability to function in different environments. To help your teen manage sensory issues, create a calm and sensory-friendly environment at home, provide sensory tools like fidget toys or noise-canceling headphones, and work with your teen's school to create a sensory-friendly learning environment.

For those with hypersensitivity, you can encourage them to wear sunglasses and/or headphones when entering environments with bright lights and loud sounds. By being aware of the textures your teen does not like, you can avoid foods and clothes that would irritate them. Help your teen find quiet spaces to work, and encourage them to socialize in areas that are not very crowded. You can also avoid using products that have very strong smells. If your teen has hyposensitivity, you can provide them with weighted blankets and food with strong textures and flavors. Teach them to take time during the day just to move, and provide them with visual aids to help them understand and retain spoken words.

Emotional Self-regulation

Emotional self-regulation is the ability to control your emotions and behavior in order to think critically, cope with daily life, and react appropriately in social situations (Omahen, 2022). Doing this effectively can be challenging for everyone, and is even more so for those with autism.

Depression

Children with ASD are four times more likely to struggle with depression, and this rate rises as they grow and become more aware of the world around them. In fact, over 70% of young people with autism experience depression, anxiety, and other mental health conditions. These symptoms often follow them into adulthood and become more severe. Genetics, dwelling on negative experiences over and over due to repetitive behaviors, and struggles with social interaction (particularly bullying and loneliness) are common factors of depression. People with ASD are also more sensitive to negative emotions and may become extremely focused on expressions of sadness and anger. Where genetics is concerned, around 40% of siblings of individuals with autism are more prone to depression, while loneliness is one of the most prominent causes of depression (Platzman-Weinstock, 2019).

There are many different symptoms of depression, including fatigue, hopelessness, an increase in repetitive and obsessive behaviors, and suicidal thoughts. It affects people's ability to communicate, engage in social events, function independently, cope with challenges, and daily life in general. There is a lot that is unknown about depression—for example, how it interacts with autism medication. More work is being done to find out the best methods for treating depression in individuals with ASD.

Anger and Meltdowns

Managing anger can be very difficult for autistic individuals. Outbursts can seem to come out of nowhere and be very surprising. There are several things that are common triggers for meltdowns.

No one likes to be ignored, and for individuals with ASD, the instinctive reaction to this is often to express their feelings in a very strong manner. Something that might seem harmless or amusing to you might come off as very offensive to someone with ASD, causing an angry reaction. Sensory overload is also a trigger, and attempting to multitask does not always end well. Order and routines help autistic individuals cope, and disruptions can result in anger. Disruptions include preventing them from doing specific activities or moving something in their space. Even being around certain people can be hard, particularly those who speak too fast, too loudly, or in high-pitched voices. Not all employers or even friends or family understand or know how to relate to autistic people, and this can lead to difficulties at work and with relationships to the point that the autistic individual becomes overcome with feelings of anger and frustration. Other factors include sleep deprivation, hunger, and the inability to adequately express themselves. All these different factors can lead to a build-up of stress. The more stressed someone is, the harder it is for them to control their anger.

Overwhelm

Your teen can get overwhelmed by difficult memories, too many sensory details, or being tired or hungry. When this happens, their chests become tight, their stomachs hurt, and it becomes all too easy for them to react to things in anger. Being overwhelmed can also bring with it feelings of confusion, dizziness, disorientation, irrationality, disassociation, and irritability. It can cause brain fog and nausea, along with chest, stomach, and neck pain, and noises rushing through their heads. Other symptoms include changes in blood pressure, trembling, and poor executive functioning. After an outburst occurs, they shut down and feel tired, and they struggle to get in touch with their emotions and process sensory information.

You can teach your teen several self-soothing techniques whenever they feel they are on the verge of a meltdown. These include encouraging them to take long walks, practicing slow breathing, and engaging in calming hobbies.

Anxiety

Around 40-50% of autistic people have received an anxiety diagnosis, with 47% experiencing severe symptoms. Anxiety is characterized by insomnia, rapid breathing, sweating, nausea, social withdrawal, and panic attacks. Other symptoms include a fast or irregular heartbeat, a sinking sensation in the stomach, and feelings of worry and restlessness. Anxiety leads to fatigue, meltdowns, and burnout, and affects the mental and physical health along with the quality of life of individuals (National Autistic Society, n.d.).

Disruption to routines and unpredictability can result in feelings of anxiety in children and adults with ASD. So too can being prevented from doing a much-loved activity, and being caught in social situations where they are unable to understand the words and emotions of the people around them. Their own thoughts and tendency to dwell on the negative things can also trigger anxiety. Some common triggers for children include being in a new environment, sensory overload, transitioning between events, and fear of things like going to sleep alone or of a particular object.

As with managing anger, anxiety is treated by first identifying triggers. Creating a journal with your child can help to track moments of anxiety and the situation surrounding these feelings. You can engage your child in cognitive behavior therapy (CBT), counseling, mindfulness training, and exposure therapy. It is important that you help your child learn to recognize when they are feeling anxious, and to employ strategies to calm themselves. Let them know that sweaty palms, an upset stomach, a racing heartbeat, hyperventilating, and flapping hands can be signs of an anxiety attack. You can use social stories and give them lots of practice on how to handle stressful situations. Using schedules, pictures, stickers, and planners is a great way to help your child manage their activities so that they feel less anxious about going places and doing things.

It is sometimes necessary to make changes to your environment to help your child feel more relaxed. Practicing deep breathing, exercising, seeking quiet spaces, and going out into nature can also help. You can encourage your child to engage in a hobby, or to use apps to help them remain calm. There are many applications geared towards children and/or adults that help them to employ self-soothing techniques to maintain their composure.

Jeremiah and the Rain

Janet Jones-Jordan is a parent advocate who runs an organization called Calculated Pathways. Her mission has been to help other parents navigate the medical and school systems for those on the autism spectrum. Her son Jeremiah is diagnosed with autism and other medical challenges. She says her son has struggled with sensitivity.

> My son likes to rub his finger up against certain surfaces, or, you know, just to feel, and the touch of certain things is a calming mechanism for him. And so in school settings… if your child has increased sensory sensations in certain environments, that's something you can put on your child's IEP so that will ensure that accommodations are in place to support your child while they're in that school setting.
>
> Find out if the child has access to sensory areas in or outside of the classroom where they can go to help calm themselves because sometimes those sensory perceptions can be so heightened it can cause the child to be frightened. It can even be painful.

Jones-Jordan mentioned a 2018 article on Spectrum News that reported that up to 90% of autistic individuals are either extremely sensitive to input from all five senses, or hardly notice them at all.

> My son has the sensitivity to rain or water coming down on his head although he absolutely loves bodies of water. I ask him (because he is verbal), 'Jeremiah, why are you so afraid of rain?' And he'll say, 'Mom, it hurts.'

It's painful, it hurts, and I've heard this before from other adults who I've encountered who have autism. They said that, you know, they've learned to cope with it. But for my son, it hurts. So we have to keep our umbrella with us at all times. On the first day of school, I give the bus driver an umbrella. I make sure the school has an umbrella, so anyone that he encounters or comes in contact with [or] that is responsible for getting him from one place to the other where he may be exposed to natural elements, I want to make sure that they have an umbrella in place.

She says she tells parents to be aware of the child's school setting including janitorial services. Sometimes those smells of the cleaning supplies are so strong it can cause a child to have sensory overload, which can lead to a meltdown. Jones-Jordan added that the World Health Organization has what's called caregiver skills training. These are strategies that you can do at home to help with your child. They're tailored specifically for a younger child. However, she was able to use some of those strategies to help her son with things like brushing his teeth and taking a shower:

Because again, that water is coming down on his head.

Transitions

Transitions often prove to be challenging for people with ASD. It requires a change from one activity to the next, which disrupts their behavioral patterns and trains of thought. This is especially challenging when they are asked to stop an activity that they are hyper-focused on, or when they are unsure of what they are supposed to do next. Poor executive function also makes transitioning more difficult, along with challenges in understanding verbal instructions.

When Nicholas was little, I always put going to the park and things he enjoyed doing on timers. And throughout the process I'd basically give him a countdown. It would be similar to "Nick, you have ten minutes left. Nick, you have five minutes left. One minute to go. Okay, it's time to go." I found if I didn't do this, we would have a meltdown. Though he is now a teenager, I still use a similar system when we are in a place that is extremely exciting or somewhere he wants to spend a lot of time. It still works.

There are several things you can do to make transitioning from one task to the next easier for your teen. Try not to just spring a transition on your child; give them plenty of time to prepare to change tasks and let them know beforehand when a transition is going to occur. When transitions become a part of your child's daily routine, they eventually fall into the habit of moving between activities. You can also alternate between giving your child a difficult task, then an easy task, and vice versa. Praise and rewards when your child successfully completes a transition will motivate them to keep working at doing so. Visual tools are particularly useful. Timers and schedules help keep them on track, and photos show them what needs to be done next. You can use checklists for them to mark off tasks, or have them place finished items into a "completion box." Whenever your child has to do an unfamiliar activity, stories and role play can help teach them what to do and how to do it.

In helping your child with transitioning from one thing to another, you equip them with skills and strategies that they can use when changing tasks at school and at work. It also reduces their stress and anxiety and improves their behavior. A lot of time can be taken up with learning how to successfully move between tasks. Knowing how to do so ensures that your child stays on schedule and is better able to focus on the task that needs to be done.

Special Interests

I have spoken before about the intense interests in specific topics or activities that individuals with autism tend to have. While these interests can be a source of joy and fulfillment, they can also be isolating and interfere with other activities.

Research carried out by Uljarević et al. (2022) showed that 75% of children with autism had at least one special interest, with 50% having two or more things that they were intensely interested in. 43% enjoyed sensory activities and regularly interacted with things that had bright colors, interesting textures, and moving parts. 19% loved trucks, cars, planes, and other vehicles, while 15% focused on cartoons, movies, and comic book characters. 13% enjoyed watching movies, and 12% had other personal interests in things such as maps, music, and many others. Some expressed interest in video games, puzzles, mechanical toys, and plants and animals. It was also seen where males were more drawn to mechanical interests while females tended to gravitate toward the creative arts. Overall, there was a marked preference in engaging in their special interests over socializing with others.

It is possible for a special interest to become so confusing that it begins to affect other areas of your teen's life. They may forget to eat or take care of themselves, and prefer to engage in their interest rather than socializing. However, there are also benefits. Being very knowledgeable about a particular field or topic can help shape their professional lives. Engaging in their interest provides them with a deep internal motivation that pushes them to pursue specific tasks, leading to learning new skills, making new discoveries, and performing well at certain projects and jobs. It brings a sense of satisfaction, completion, and accomplishment, and can raise their self-esteem and build valuable life skills.

To help your teen balance their special interests with other activities, set limits on screen time, encourage physical activity or outdoor play, and offer alternative activities that align with their interests.

ANGER MANAGEMENT WITH DARRYL AND JABAAR

Jabaar Hassan is a 31-year-old adult on the autism spectrum. His caregiver is his cousin Darryl Price, who explained that Jabaar has and has had issues with bullying in the past. Price explained first that when Jabaar's dad died, the family wanted to put him in a home, but Jabaar wanted to stay in the house that his dad built and be around family.

> So [I] took on the responsibility and I told his dad before he died, he didn't have to worry about Jabaar. We've been like little brothers since he was born.

Price mentioned that Jabaar often has to travel by bus to locations because he doesn't feel he's quite ready to drive yet. He said that sometimes he worries about Jabaar when he's at the bus stop or bus station.

> There's a lot of homeless people, people that you know, can tell that he has autism and they may try to take advantage of him, pick on him, just like they did when he was in high school.

He says he constantly reminds Jabaar to put up all valuables including his phone and money, especially in high school where there were often people who would pick on the weakest person in the class. That just happened to be Jabaar. This was something that kept Jabaar in trouble. Price said right around high school graduation, a teen picked on him in the cafeteria, and Jabaar did the right thing.

> He went to the teacher to report it, and the teacher didn't do anything. So with his autism, he has a little bit of anger management. And so when the kid just got him to the brink of getting angry, he struck out. He struck out at the teacher because the teacher didn't pay attention to the fact that he was telling them he was being picked on, and so that got him in trouble.

> They wouldn't let him walk for his graduation ceremony with all the other teenagers in his class.

They put him out. They actually would let him walk a day later with some other kids, and we thought that was very unfair to him because they knew his situation and so forth.

Price says his family had put Jabaar in Karate, and he has a brown belt.

That's why he has to curtail his anger management. Because I tell him all the time [that] at your age, you're responsible for everything you do, no matter your situation. So you have to basically control your anger—no matter how angry you get.

Sometimes I tell him to picture me saying just calm down, walk away, and relax so that he doesn't get upset because he actually becomes the Hulk when he gets upset. But he's a very sweet person, very well-mannered...

Bullying

Teens with autism are more likely to be victims of bullying than their neurotypical peers. Bullying can take many forms including exclusion from activities, name-calling and insults, physical attacks, and taking away a person's things. It can sometimes be difficult to tell if your child is being bullied, particularly if they are nonverbal. Sometimes teens internalize their experiences and feel ashamed of themselves. They feel as if they deserve to be bullied, or they do not know how to share what is happening to them. Some feel that talking to an adult about being bullied will make them more hated by their peers. There are also autistic teens who are completely unaware that they are being bullied.

While knowing if your child has been bullied can be hard, there are some clues that can help. For example, your child may come home with cuts and bruises. They may be hungry even though you gave them lunch or lunch money, and some of their personal items might be missing. Their academic performance might suffer, and they may resist going to school. Traveling to places on their own might become something very difficult and scary for them. Your teen might become more aggressive, anxious, and withdrawn, and may stammer a lot. They may cry more; experience stomach aches, mood swings, and nightmares; and refuse to talk about what is happening to them. Some may even start bullying others.

To help your teen avoid bullying, teach them self-advocacy skills, work with their school to create a safe and inclusive learning environment, and seek support from local autism organizations or bullying prevention resources like StopBullying.gov. Sites like these help children and parents recognize signs of bullying, and provide resources and strategies on how to manage it.

It is very important that you listen to your teen and show them that you care. Make them feel comfortable talking to you and try to remain calm. For those with nonverbal ASD, you can ask them to tell you what is happening by drawing pictures, or touching happy, sad, angry, scared, and so on faces while you ask them how they feel about various things (for example, asking them about lunch, specific classes, morning and evening activities, etc.).

Bullying is never the victim's fault, and this is something that you should help your child to understand. You can create a safe social environment for your teen by planning social events for them to meet and build connections with other teens. Help your child to understand what bullying is and how to handle it. You can use stories, videos, images, songs, and role play to teach them how to remain calm, walk away from the situation, find a safe space, and report the incident to an adult.

Be sure to get in contact with your child's school rather than trying to handle it on your own. You can work with the school to promote autism awareness, and to provide alternate spaces or supervision for moments when your child needs to leave the classroom—whether it is to have lunch, go to the bathroom, or other activities. The school can also appoint a member of staff as a point of communication for the students to report bullying. An anonymous report system can also be set up so that students can feel comfortable reporting their experiences.

If you discover that your child is bullying others, one of the first steps is to find out the trigger behind their behavior. Help them to understand what they are doing, the consequences, and how it makes others feel. You can again work with the school to direct your teen's energy into different meaningful activities, and to teach them social skills. Rewards for good behavior will also help.

Mental Health

I have spoken about how teens with autism are more prone to depression and anxiety along with other mental health conditions. This is due to several factors such as difficulty coping with academics, socialization, and daily life; knowledge that they are different from their peers; and the tendency to dwell on negative thoughts.

Some signs of mental health struggles that your teen might display are fatigue and unwillingness to do simple daily activities—even ones they used to do before. They may become more withdrawn, display increased aggressiveness, and show drastic changes in their sleeping and eating patterns. Compulsive and repetitive behaviors may also increase. Teens may begin to self-harm, and their conversations may become more centered on suicide and death.

If you notice that your child is having challenges with their mental health, sit them down in a calm, safe, nonjudgmental environment and talk to them. Show them love and understanding, and ask questions that are clear and direct. Do not pressure them to answer. Instead, let them know that you are listening, and they can take the time to think about it and gather their thoughts.

To support your teen's mental health, seek out counseling or therapy services, teach coping skills like mindfulness or relaxation techniques, and work with your teen's healthcare provider to manage symptoms. You can engage them in a hobby, and ensure that they exercise, stay hydrated, and eat healthy. Spending time in nature is a big help. When your child displays negative thoughts about themselves, you can help them to think about the positive things in their life and the people who love and support them.

CHAPTER 3

DAY-TO-DAY DILEMMAS

What's normal for the spider is a calamity for the fly.
–Morticia Addams

AVERY'S HAIRCUT

I had the pleasure of interviewing LaChan V. Hannon, Ph.D., who is the executive director of Greater Expectations Teaching and Advocacy. She is also the Director of Teacher Preparation & Innovation in the Department of Urban Education at Rutgers-Newark.

Hannon has an adult son, Avery, on the autism spectrum who is attending college. She shared with me a few stories. One story was about cultural pushback from relatives after she and her husband noticed some delays with her son when he was 5.

> He wasn't developing his language like his sister, and he and his sister are only 19 months apart.
>
> He was a quiet kid and I'm thinking, well, maybe he can't hear. I mean, mind you, we were in a house with a lot of people and there were multiple children. It was a loud house, and he just was so unbothered. So we were getting his hearing tested. [The doctor told us]

'No, his hearing is fine' and I'm like, 'Are you sure? Like, something's not how I remember this..being with my daughter.'

[We] went through two and three rounds of different audiologists and tests and they're like, nothing is wrong with his hearing. I'm like, OK. So then we start to see some of the repetitive behaviors, and we start to see some of the stemming though we didn't have the word for it back then. And I'm like, 'We need to call early intervention.' So we called the early interventionist. When the early interventionist said what she thought it might be, I already knew. And then we just kicked it into high gear from there.

I asked if she received any pushback from family who she may have thought were supporting her efforts

Yeah, absolutely. I remember I wrote a chapter in a book for a colleague of mine a couple of years ago, and there's a section in that chapter that's called 'Ain't nothing wrong with that boy.' And so it was really that chapter, while I focused on—I think—interactions that I have with my grandmother, that was the general sentiment.

My husband and I decided that we had to set some firmer boundaries with family. And so if I say he doesn't do something after 8:00, I said what I said, right? And if you can't respect that then we have to set some additional boundaries. And so for a while, we weren't around. We were very much insular in our home, in our nucleus, doing our thing.

I asked: What advice would you have for parents who are struggling with this, trying to get their kids prepared for being an adult? And I'm sure you've, you know what I'm talking about.

> Practice muscle memory. I mean, and it's not only helpful for him, it's helpful for us. Right? It's like I'm not trying to traumatize you in any way, shape, or form, but the next time you go to look for your favorite fork, it's not going to be there. How are you gonna improvise?
>
> That's how we've been able to be most successful; by trying to keep things as routine as possible, but also allowing for flexibility. And so, sometimes there are planned mistakes, sometimes there are mistakes that aren't planned. Sometimes it's just talking through. Well, what would you do if the peanut butter wasn't here? What would you do? What could you do? What else could you do? What else could you eat? What else could you make? And practicing those.
>
> My son is a freshman at Temple University living in a dorm with the roommate he met when they first moved in. And next semester he's like 'I want to live in an apartment'. I was like, 'You mean with a stove? Like you mean with a stove like a real stove with a real kitchen? Not like you go to the dining hall?' He's like, 'Yeah, yeah, I want to learn how to take care of myself better'. And guess what we'll be doing this summer? Cooking all summer, and that makes me feel safer, right? It makes him feel safer. You have to get into the habit of not always having what you need in order to do the thing.

I asked her: Does he have executive functioning challenges?

> I can tell you every place he's been in the house, as he has walked through it, because nothing is the way that I left it. Now, mind you, my brother lives in Philly, so I'm like, ask your uncle where you can get a haircut. He Ubers all the way back to the town that we live in, gets his haircut, and then Ubers back. I'm like, 'So you spend $120 on a $20.00 haircut. All you had to do was ask somebody.'

> But in his mind, he was—'I took care of it. I did it by myself. I didn't need any help.'

> And I'm like, 'And now you're broke, right?' And he says, 'So but you can't be mad. And I reply, 'I can be mad that you don't have any money. Now it's not how I would have solved it, and now we can offer some suggestions… But don't ever spend $120.00 on a haircut.'

EXECUTIVE FUNCTIONING

Executive functioning is a set of cognitive skills that are involved in planning, organizing, and carrying out tasks. These skills allow individuals to set goals, create plans to achieve those goals, monitor their progress, and adjust their behavior as needed. It involves several key skills, including:

- **Working memory**: the ability to hold information in your mind for a short period of time while you use it to complete a task
- **Attention**: sustaining focus on a task or goal, while filtering out distractions

- **Inhibition**: the ability to control impulses or resist distractions when needed
- **Cognitive flexibility**: being able to adjust to changing situations, switch between tasks, and adapt to new information
- **Planning and organization**: the ability to create a plan for completing a task, and to organize materials and resources to carry out that plan
- **Problem-solving**: knowing how to identify a problem, generate possible solutions, and select the best solution to the problem
- **Self-regulation**: the ability to regulate emotions and behavior in response to a situation and to monitor and adjust your own behavior to achieve a goal

Executive functioning is essential for success in many areas of life, including academic achievement, social interactions, and daily living skills. Individuals with executive functioning difficulties may struggle with completing tasks, following through on instructions, regulating their emotions, and adapting to new situations.

Teens on the spectrum may encounter difficulties with the following:

- **Time management**: Teens with autism may struggle with managing their time effectively. They may have trouble estimating how long tasks will take or struggle to prioritize tasks.
- **Planning and organization**: They may have trouble breaking down complex tasks into smaller steps or struggle to create a plan for completing a task.
- **Difficulty with working memory**: Teens with autism may have trouble holding information in their working memory, which can impact their ability to follow instructions or complete tasks.
- **Attention and focus**: Some teens may struggle with sustaining attention and focusing on tasks, which can make it difficult

to complete tasks or follow through on instructions. A woman who has autism explained to me when I commented on my son's challenge with staying on task with homework that there's something called time blindness. This is when someone just loses track of time during a task.

- **Flexibility and adapting to change**: They may have trouble adapting to changes in routine or unexpected events, which can impact their ability to complete tasks or adjust to new situations.
- **Decision-making**: Making decisions can be a struggle, especially when there are multiple options or the consequences of the decision are uncertain.
- **Self-regulation**: Some may have trouble regulating their emotions or controlling impulsive behavior, which can impact their ability to complete tasks or interact with others appropriately.
- **Problem-solving**: They may struggle to identify and solve problems, especially when the problems are complex or require abstract thinking.
- **Initiating tasks**: Teens with autism may have trouble getting started on tasks or may need extra support to begin tasks.
- **Completing tasks**: Some teens may struggle to complete tasks, especially when the tasks are long or complex.

Tips on How to Improve Your Teen's Executive Functioning

To help teens with autism improve their executive functioning skills, it can be helpful to keep the communication lines open as best you can. Sometimes your teen may seem as if they do not want to talk, when in reality they just do not know how to approach you about certain topics. They may also take time to respond to you as they try to process what you have said and how they want to respond. You can make this easier for them by starting the conversation yourself and being patient while they think of how to reply. However, there is a time and place for conversation. Your child might be too distracted, overwhelmed, or just not ready to talk about certain things. Consider their feelings and state of mind before initiating certain conversational topics.

There may be times when you need to shift conversational gears and talk about their interests. This will capture their attention and allow them to engage you in discussion on something they are knowledgeable and passionate about. Over time, your teen will become more comfortable talking to you and more receptive to discussing other topics. It is also important to remember that, while your teen may be growing, they still have some maturing to do. They do not have your experiences, and they respond to things differently, so be sure to keep their mental and physical age in mind when talking to them. Teens—especially autistic teens—may lash out or react in hurtful ways. It can be tempting to take this personally, but try not to do so. Instead, practice empathy, patience, and understanding even though this can be challenging for you when they say or do certain things.

You can also provide them with structured routines and clear expectations. Encourage your child to take breaks and break down tasks into smaller steps. Visual or written instructions can be used to help your child understand what is expected of them. You can also use visual aids such as checklists or calendars to help with time management and organization. Your teen can benefit from using coping strategies such as deep breathing or mindfulness to help with self-regulation. Identify their specific triggers and have plans in place to help them calm down fast.

ORGANIZATION WITH RACHEL WILLIAMS

Social worker Rachel Williams and I spoke further on helping kids with executive functioning in school. She mentioned the various strategies she uses in helping them with being organized.

> That is a challenging piece for a lot of our kids, more challenging than others, definitely helping

them stay organized. [One thing that has helped is] using folders—colored folders. [We say] okay, this is your English folder. This is your math folder. [We also try to get] the child in a routine of… okay, now when we're done with homework, we're gonna put our books in our book bag. And now we're gonna put our book bag by the door so we don't forget our book bag.

So routine, structure—lots of structure—and sort of like almost like training them to do things a certain way because that's gonna become very important when they get to the high school level and even at the college level. You know, even for kids who aren't on the spectrum, you know, just being organized and having good time management skills. I find a lot of kids need [help with this].

She noted that some school systems can provide an aide or in-class support for your child if they need it.

If the child has an in-class support, he/she is extremely instrumental. I work closely with the in-class support teachers because I have a lot of students that are in the main building.

In Ms. Williams' school, some of the children in the special needs programs are in an annex building where additional services are provided. The main building is where the mainstreamed and transitional children learn.

And so part of what we do together is making sure, okay, did the child pack up the homework cause they may say, well, they didn't do their homework last night. It's the teacher assistant that is doing these

things and making sure you know, okay, you have
[what you need] and then they put everything in
like Google, you know, Google Classroom and just
reviewing that with the student, making sure, okay,
you have homework tonight in English, let's make sure
we bring your English book home.

She said she's seen where a teacher and aide went as far as having
two sets of texts: one for home and another for school so the child can
keep up with work. Usually, if a child is going to be mainstreamed
from middle school to high school, the teacher will set up things so
that the student gets used to changing classrooms so that they are used
to it by the time they get to high school.

And so they've set up their program where they will
switch classrooms amongst one another. And so [the
child's] gonna have to remember: ohh I need this
book for this class because I'm now going to this class.
He may even have a locker where he could become
better organized. So all of that helps. The teacher
assistants, the in-class support teachers... they're
very instrumental in making sure the child stays
organized.

Ms. Williams also spoke about some concerns that she goes over
with her students in helping them to stay organized.

I have a list of concerns that I review with my in-class
support kids and we go over it and we come up with
a plan. Why didn't you do your homework? You have
a project next week. When are you gonna get started?
And sometimes we'll even start some of these projects,
just brainstorming ideas. They need a lot of assistance
with brainstorming for ideas when dealing with larger
projects.

I asked her if she found that some kids had a problem when she talks about in-classroom supports. She told me it's not uncommon that some students may be embarrassed.

> Sometimes those who need less support may be more socially aware of what is going on. They want to be included like everyone else or a 'typical teenager'. And I mean, what we just stress to the child is that listen, the in-class support teachers are not just for you, they're for everybody, you know, in the classroom and really that is their role.

She added letting the kids feel that they are not alone, showing and teaching the benefits of having that additional teacher and why they're important, is often helpful.

> I think it's still very important, but you know allowing this child to feel confident and feel like he or she can do certain things independently, we encourage that.

HELPING YOUR TEEN MANAGE AND UNDERSTAND THEMSELVES

Personal Hygiene

This is a big one for parents. I honestly refuse to have a big stinky teenager in my home. I have made it a major part of Nick's routine since he was little about schedules for showers, brushing and flossing his teeth, and wearing deodorant. Oh, the need for deodorant! And honestly it comes down to routine. Nick has been resistant at times, but knows I will keep sending him back to the bathroom until he does it. Written schedules and visual tools honestly do help.

Schedules and visual tools are a great way to teach your child how to take care of their body. You can break down tasks into steps, and teach your child how and when to do hygienic tasks. For example, you can create checklists detailing steps on how to brush their teeth, comb their hair, etc. when they wake up. These checklists can be placed in places such as on the bathroom mirror, and include images of people completing each step. Consider your child's needs and understanding when creating these schedules. Some teens need multiple steps, while others struggle when faced with too many. You might find that simply saying "brush your teeth" is not enough, and you may need to list out the steps of getting the items, wetting the toothbrush, applying toothpaste, and brushing the outside, tops, then sides, etc. of their teeth.

Videos and social stories are other tools that you can use to help your child practice good hygiene. You can use commercial videos and stories, or video yourself performing actions and share stories of how you take care of your body. Social stories are particularly helpful when told in the first person, as it helps your teen put themselves into the shoes of the character. These stories can begin by talking about noticing a problem—for example, smelling an odor or feeling sticky— and then describing the steps taken to address the problem.

If your child is nonverbal, you can provide them with a sign that they can use to let people know when they need to use the bathroom. Sometimes your teen may struggle to understand their body and realize when they need to relieve themselves, and this can lead to accidents. A great way to help with this is to establish a set daily routine. By training them to go to the bathroom at certain times, you will help them develop a habit that will ensure their needs are taken care of, even when they do not feel as if they have to go. You can also use timing to ensure that they wash themselves properly. For example, they can be told to bathe for at least 10 minutes, to rub their hands together at least 10 times when washing their hands, and so on. Alarms and timers can be used as reminders of when to perform a hygienic activity.

You should also keep in mind any sensitivities that your child may have. Perhaps the bathroom lighting needs to be dimmed, and unnecessary distractions, especially loud noises, removed. Some towels and other toiletries may be too rough on the skin or have smells that are too strong. You can provide your child with a variety of options of items to use such as tissues, wipes, and fabric and paper towels. It is also very important that you do the tasks with your teen, providing guidance and encouragement, then slowly step back and allow them to take care of themselves independently. Giving rewards whenever your teen accomplishes a task will help them to feel a sense of satisfaction and motivate them to continue practicing proper hygiene.

Stimming

When Nick was much younger, he used to spin. He loved twirling in circles and on a toy called the Sit n' Spin. That toy was his go-to for long periods of time. It seemed to soothe him. He's grown out of that. And today his go-to is self-talk. We've had conversations about learning how to keep self-talk at home and quiet. For Nick, I believe self-talk is a way of working through things in his head and emotions. Usually after a long session in his room, Nick will come out and talk to me at length about something he's experienced at school or a video he's watched online to figure it all out. It's his way of processing all the information and emotions associated with the experience. Many children move into adolescence with stimming of different types.

However, stimming can also have negative effects on your child's life. Some actions—such as hair-pulling, scratching at skin, and hand-biting—can lead to injury. It can also be disruptive if your child is constantly opening and closing doors and turning lights on and off. In paying attention to their movements, your child might miss valuable information in class and social cues.

You can help your child manage stimming by teaching them to seek out calmer environments when they are feeling anxious. Fidget toys, music, and certain textures can also give them something to interact with in a quieter way. If your child's stimming is harmful or negatively impacts their general life, you can also seek help from medical professionals.

One common stimming activity that people with autism engage

in is self-talk. In general, people have moments when they make comments to themselves. However, for people with autism, this may occur more frequently and subconsciously. Self-talk occurs for many reasons. Your teen may talk to themselves when they are bored, struggle to understand lessons in class, or experience feelings of anxiety, nervousness, or excitement. They may also self-talk when rehearsing upcoming activities and conversations, struggling to recall something, or to help to ensure that they are following the steps in a sequence.

If self-talking is disruptive, there are ways you can help your child to manage this. If this occurs during the classroom, you can work with the class teacher to come up with ways to keep your child motivated and engaged. Teaching your teen how to read social cues and engage in conversation with others will also help. You can show them how to choose quiet activities to alleviate boredom, or suggest that they listen to music as a means of distracting and centering themselves.

Keeping Their Spaces in Order

Having a cluttered, unclean space can be very difficult for teens with ASD. However, achieving this is equally challenging due to struggles with organization. This makes helping your teen organize their surroundings and maintaining a cleaning routine very important. Many of the strategies—using visual aids, breaking down tasks, modeling—that I have already mentioned are useful in teaching your teen how to keep their space clean. Here is another strategy that may seem strange but actually works: combining messes. You can gather the messy items in your teen's room and place them in one area. That way, they know that this is what needs to be tidied up so that their room will be clean. It helps them to learn to distinguish between what is clean and what is untidy. Labels and containers can also be used to help keep things organized. It is also important that you use visual aids, schedules, routines, and modeling to help your child in doing chores.

Transportation

Millions of children face a trial every morning as they go to school: the school bus. This can be very scary for children with autism. The students can be rowdy, and your child cannot simply leave the bus. Riding on the bus comes with a whole different set of rules, and they have to listen to the bus driver. There are also a lot of unknowns: routes, buses, and drivers may change, and the flow of traffic influences the journey. You can use social stories to help prepare your child for the bus ride before the school year begins. Model what to do in various possible situations regarding the ride, and give your child lots of opportunities to practice. You can encourage your child to listen to music or give them fidget toys to help them manage sensory overload and their emotions.

If your child experiences bullying, reach out to the bus driver, teacher, or other member of staff. Let your child know that there are people they can go to for help. Some schools allow you to have a trial run on the bus to see how your child handles it. You can also include bus accommodations when discussing your child's individualized education program with the school. It might help to introduce your child to the bus driver before they travel on the bus, and to provide the driver with information on your child—for example, sensory challenges, likes, dislikes, and strategies to prevent and manage meltdowns. Taking the bus was added to my child's IEP so that he could get used to riding with large groups, sounds, and following directions. It's helped him tremendously.

When preparing your child to travel, it is best to do so when they are young. Take them with you as you run errands and go on trips using public transportation, and explicitly model how to behave and what to do. Be sure to break down and verbalize things as you do them. Teach your child how to read bus schedules and maps, and suggest ways they can occupy themselves as they wait for the bus or train. These could include reading, listening to music, drawing, or playing with a fidget toy.

Learning to drive has become a well-established part of growing up. However, the sensory input that comes with driving can be overwhelming. It is important that you consider things such as your teen's cognitive ability and flexibility, attention, planning, motor skills, emotional regulation, and judgment before determining if it is safe for them to learn to drive. You can work with the school to come up with strategies to teach your child how to drive, as well as seek professional help. Try not to just force your child into learning; it may be safer to have them use other forms of transportation.

Beyond Graduation

The transition between high school/college and the working world is not easy, and this is even more so for individuals with ASD. It requires a change in lifestyle and the loss of established routines. Children with autism often need some extra help to be prepared for this transition in their lives.

You can help your teen by being open about their diagnosis, what it means, and how it will affect them. Symptoms may change over time, so you can request that your child's evaluation be updated. Self-acceptance is crucial. Let your child know that there is nothing wrong with being different. Teach them to love and appreciate themselves, and show them that you love and are proud of them.

As parents and caregivers, it is important to present a united front with your child. Keep the lines of communication open with your partner, medical professionals, and school staff. Open, face-to-face communication with your child is also important. As your child grows, they should be allowed more input in important life decisions. Eventually, your role will lessen and you will become more of a guide and advice-giver when they ask.

It is quite typical for teens to resist taking advice from their parents. If that is the case, you can help your child build a connection with someone trustworthy whom they are willing to listen to and go to for help. The teenage years can be difficult, so be prepared for outbursts and angst. Rather than fighting over everything, allow your teen reasonable freedom while setting boundaries.

Proper planning is essential for ensuring that your child is comfortable, performing to their fullest potential, and independent.

Be sure to discuss academic and job options with your child. Knowing their triggers, special interests, strengths, and weaknesses will help in crafting goals and the steps that need to be taken to achieve these goals. In addition to individualized education plans (IEPs), there are also 504 plans offered under the Rehabilitation Act. 504s protect your child's rights and help them to receive fair educational access. You can request a 504 to help your child in school.

Not all teens and young adults with ASD are ready to live on campus after being accepted to college. In deciding their residency, have a discussion with your child, and look at their experiences going to camp or staying over with friends and family. It is also okay to request a delay in graduating if your child needs extra support.

There are many soft skills that your child may need to be explicitly taught, and it is best if this begins while they are still young. Knowing when they need help, where to go, and how to ask for it are necessary skills for your child to learn. You can also engage your child in social groups and volunteering activities. In doing so, you can help them to find social spaces where they are comfortable, and help them to practice empathy. There are also some part-time jobs that make accommodations for teens with special needs.

Consider applying for social security disability insurance once your child turns 18. It is also important to ensure that legal and financial steps are taken to protect your child in case something happens. You can set up a savings-plan with your teen. Your child needs your love, support, guidance, and patience as they grow from babies into adulthood. Try to be there for them and build a support network that both you and they can rely on.

In an upcoming chapter, we will talk about employment opportunities for individuals with ASD.

CHAPTER 4

THE SOCIAL TEEN

Being a teenager is an amazing time and a hard time. It's when you make your best friends—I have girls who will never leave my heart and I still talk to. You get the best and the worst as a teen. You have the best friendships and the worst heartbreaks.
—Sophia Bush

SOCIAL CUES WITH DR. DURR

Dr. Angel Durr is a data scientist and professor at the University of Nevada. She also is an Afro-Latina on the autism spectrum. We spoke about her life as a teen in school.

> I was labeled as shy instead of autistic, and so people just thought I didn't like to talk, but it was really just me watching people and studying their behavior and understanding how to engage and watching a lot of TV and stuff like that so that I could learn what normal social engagement looks like.
>
> I had a lot of disabled friends growing up because we just got each other and in that, there was a lot of camaraderie. But I feel like nowadays I see a lot of

stuff online and I feel like kids are very welcoming towards kids with disabilities and they'll bring them into the fold. And that really wasn't something that happened when I was a younger person. It was more of like you're ostracized. And so I never really had a group where I fit in. And that was really a struggle for me, and it was probably even more of a struggle for my mom, who also had autism. She got into a lot of groups with bad kids because of that.

AUTISM AND SOCIAL CHALLENGES

Social interactions can be very tricky. There are a lot of written and unwritten rules regarding how to communicate with others. Having social skills is all about knowing these rules and having the ability to navigate social situations. Examples of social skills include active listening, co-operation, empathy, conflict resolution, giving and receiving feedback, and patience. Some of these are explicitly taught to us, but we pick up a lot as we grow and interact with others. For individuals with autism, it can feel as if they are playing a guessing game where everyone else knows the rules and expects them to know them as well. They want to connect with others, but don't just quite know how to do it, and this can lead to social isolation. Because of this, children and teens with ASD need a little help in socializing.

As children age into teens, social withdrawal tends to worsen. Around 20% of teens with ASD are left out of activities, more than 40% only ever saw their friends while at school, and 54% had friends who never called them (Sarris, 2013).

Some common challenges faced by children with autism are:

- Difficulty reading social cues: Individuals with autism may have difficulty interpreting nonverbal cues such as facial expressions, body language, and tone of voice, which are essential for understanding social situations.

- Lack of social reciprocity: Autistic individuals may struggle to understand the give-and-take nature of social interactions, and may have difficulty taking turns or sharing the conversation.
- Difficulty with abstract language: Things commonly used in social interactions such as sarcasm, irony, or figurative language are difficult to understand for individuals with ASD.
- Sensory sensitivities: Hyper- or hypo-sensivity can make social situations overwhelming or uncomfortable.
- Anxiety and social phobia: Social situations can be anxiety-provoking for individuals with autism, especially if they have experienced negative social interactions in the past.

These challenges can make it difficult for teens and tweens on the autism spectrum to connect with peers and build positive social relationships. However, with support and guidance, many autistic individuals are able to improve their social skills and build meaningful connections with others.

IMPROVING YOUR TEEN'S SOCIAL SKILLS

Every parent of a child, teen, or adult on the spectrum often says be patient when it comes to building social skills with your child. It takes time. And like a muscle, it needs to be exercised and flexed.

To help your teen build social connections, consider enrolling them in social skills groups or encouraging them to join clubs or activities that align with their interests. Social groups for teens with autism can be found through local autism organizations or through online resources like Meetup. Meetup is a social media site that helps individuals find and connect with groups that share similar interests. It allows groups to schedule online and in-person events, get more involved in their communities, and spend more time engaging in hobbies and interests (GCF Global, n.d.).

Social skills groups are usually taught by professionals such as general education and specialized teachers, behavioral and occupational therapists, and school psychologists. These groups carefully break down social interactions and skills into small steps and use simple language with lots of concrete examples. You often have to vet these groups and figure out if it's a right fit. It's not a plug-and-play kind of thing. Parents have told me—and in my experience—finding a group who has a mix of multicultural members who allow the child to connect as well as the parents to connect is a delicate balance. A good social skills group is well-structured and consistent, and allows teens to collaborate with each other. Teens should be given multiple opportunities to practice their skills in different contexts. The group should also work at building the self-esteem and awareness of its members. You can also engage your child in functional communication training that teaches them to stop and use appropriate gestures and words in asking for things or expressing a feeling instead of going straight into a meltdown.

There are many different things you can teach your teen to help improve how they interact with others. For example, you can teach them how to discreetly observe conversations, identify what the group is talking about, and then wait until there is a break in the talking to move closer and add to the topic. Teach them how to observe personal space and to take turns in speaking. Knowing how to leave conversations and to say sorry when a mistake is made are also important.

You can teach your teen the rules of electronic etiquette, how to use humor appropriately, and how to organize hang-outs. Other very useful social skills for your teen include knowing how to identify possible friend groups and how to deal with pressure, rejection, and conflict amongst their peers.

Children with autism tend to have deep interests in certain facts and activities and spend a lot of time engaging in these things. You can teach your child that their interests can be used as conversational topics. There are people out there who are interested in the same things, and this creates a common ground that can be used to interact with others.

Many teens and children with ASD struggle to focus, and this can lead to them missing things in conversation, going off topic, or getting bored and abruptly leaving conversations. Fidget toys can provide them with stimulation to help them focus. You can also teach them to actively listen by maintaining eye contact and waiting for pauses to ask questions.

Spoken language can be hard to interpret for people with autism, particularly those with a delay in language development. And some children with ASD are non-verbal. Jane Brobbey is a mom of an autistic young adult who is non-verbal. She explained in an interview that for years teachers told her that her child was intellectually challenged because he couldn't speak. She noticed her son Kwame would point to pictures she posted on her refrigerator to communicate what he wanted. But when educators would evaluate him, using pictures on a flat horizontal surface, he could not identify the pictures or communicate with the evaluator. She just couldn't understand why and what was going on until she attended a seminar to teach parents with non-verbal children to use tablets and spelling for communication. During that time, she learned about a condition where some diagnosed with autism cannot read on comprehend words, pictures or information easily on a horizontal flat surface. The difficulty has to do with visual orientation (or position of their head when reading). However, if the information is presented vertically or at a different angle, the person can comprehend and communicate.

Brobbey says at first she didn't believe this applied to her son but when she brought home the material, he began spelling words she didn't know he understood. She was shocked. Today, she homeschools Kwame who is 21 years old. He is completing his high school education this year and plans to attend college classes online. He is also in an advanced reading club and has expressed he wants to be a writer. Brobbey has since written her own book called: No More School Bus to share with other parents ways to teach their children independently at home.

Helping your child navigate may mean you need to use technology, pictures, music, charts, and role play to teach them about your experiences in school, at restaurants, at the doctor and more.

These visual tools can be used to break down and demonstrate tasks. Making it interactive, visually eye-catching, and fun will help your child understand better, engage their interest, and make it easier for them to remember what you have taught. Using stories and modeling from peers can make learning social skills more relatable and easier to understand.

Encouraging autistic teens to communicate their needs and feelings can help them build stronger relationships with peers. Try to teach your child problem-solving skills, as these can help them learn how to navigate social conflicts and challenges. Building your teens self-esteem can also help them feel more confident in social situations and more willing to take risks and try new things. Be sure to provide feedback and positive reinforcement for appropriate social behavior, as doing so can help your child feel more confident and motivated to continue practicing their social skills.

HELPING YOUR TEEN WITH RELATIONSHIPS

Teen relationships are a territory that honestly I am just starting with when it comes to my own teenager. The information I'm sharing is purely from research, and my personal stories in this area are limited. I do however want to say from a personal perspective helping my teen with relationships has been something I've addressed throughout his childhood. We always talk about appropriate and inappropriate language, touch, and conversations. I have always allowed him to ask questions and try to never shut him down so that he feels comfortable sharing.

Feelings of attraction occur in your autistic teen the same way as with any other teenager. Your child may, however, need some help in understanding what they feel and how to handle it. I have spoken about the usefulness of social stories, modeling, and visual aids, and they can be applied in this situation. You can help your child understand the physical reactions that come with attraction—for example, elevated heart-beat, changes in breathing, a tingly feeling, and so on.

Understanding how someone feels about you is challenging. You can use pictures, videos, and modeling to help your child figure out when someone might be attracted to them, or uninterested. It is crucial that you teach your child how to respond—whether to suggest a friendship, attempt to pursue a relationship, give a polite rejection, or move on. Learning how to handle rejection is also important. Teach your child to accept the word "no," and to use the word themselves when they are feeling uncomfortable or do not reciprocate someone's feelings. It is important to let your child know that a rejection does not mean that there is something wrong with them. There are many reasons why people say no, and it in no way diminishes your child's importance and value.

Rather than jumping straight into a romantic relationship, encourage your teen to first build a friendship and find common interests. Help them to learn how to clearly express what they feel, stand up for themselves, and be considerate of the feelings and needs of the other person. You can also help your child to understand, respect, and maintain personal boundaries. If your child is nervous about spending one-on-one time with someone they are attracted to, you can suggest they begin with a group date. This will help them to become more comfortable with and learn more about the person.

You may be tempted to hover and protect your child from heartbreak. However, at some point you need to step back and let your child make their own decisions, even if it means they end up getting hurt.

Sensory input can pose a challenge while dating. Help your child understand that it is okay to not want to be touched, and that there are other people who feel the same. You can also help them become more comfortable by practicing sitting close to them, touching their arm, or hugging them. When doing this, be aware of your child's boundaries and do not force them to accept physical contact.

Be sure to teach your child the signs of a healthy and unhealthy relationship. The following questions are things to look at:

Is the person honest? Are they ashamed of or taking advantage of you? Do they support you? Do they force you to do things? Are they also happy with doing things you like? Does the person hurt or bully you?

Breakups are another thing your teen may need help with. Try to be there for them, and encourage them to write down their feelings, spend time with family, socialize, and engage in hobbies. Be patient with them as they process their post-breakup feelings.

HAVING "THE SEX TALK" WITH NICK

The sex talk with my son is an ongoing process. My advice to any parent who is doing this with their special needs child is to gauge how much information to disclose because it's confusing enough for a neurotypical teen, much more for a child on the spectrum. Nicholas is the kind of kid who will just directly ask. And over the years I have learned not to respond with horror or shock but just think logically how to explain things in a very technical and scientific way so that he gets it. Also, I have tried my best to inject a gentleness and easy tone throughout our conversations so that he understands that sex is not all technical and parts—there are feelings and emotions involved. And that he can share with me or his dad questions about anything.

One conversation I recall went something like this:

Nick: "Did you and dad have sex?"

Me: "Yes. That's how you got here."

Nick: "Yeah. People have sex to have babies. But I read that sometimes people have sex not just to have a baby?"

Me: "Yes, that happens."

Nick: "Oh—" (with an embarrassed look on his face) "Did you and dad do that?"

Me: "Yes. Why do you ask?"

Nick: "Wow. Ok. 'Cause we talked about it in health class. Did you use condoms and stuff?

Me: "Sometimes."

Nick: "Why? I thought you had sex to have me?"

Me: "We did. But sex isn't just to have babies. Your dad and I love each other. And that was something we did in our private time after we were married. We waited until a special time to have you because we wanted to have enough time and money to take care of you. Sex is a big responsibility. Did you have any more questions? You can ask me anything."

Nick: "Yeah, I learned about it in health class. And you gave me that book. I know all that other stuff. I just wanted to ask you."

I have had these conversations about girls, anatomy, wet dreams, and why things work the way they do in different ways. I've had to explain a few times that different venues in public weren't appropriate places to have conversations. After a few times, Nick finally understood that talking about sensitive sexual topics at a restaurant or in a public shopping mall wasn't the appropriate spot for discussion. My husband and I have often had a good laugh after questions. But we encourage him to ask, because we believe it is important for him to be comfortable asking and sharing with us any questions about intimacy and sex so that he won't feel uncomfortable. And I want him well-informed.

I've taken conversations slow. And allowed him often to lead the conversation with a question.

And given the current political climate about the LGBTQ + community, we have gotten plenty of questions about this. Honestly, I have had to break out my phone and google a lot of terms like "pansexual" to explain. And most of the time, Nick is very matter-of-fact about what he has learned and what some of his friends have declared to him. And with every conversation, I have tried to remain neutral, allowing him to make up his mind about where he fits in the world.

SEX AND RELATIONSHIPS

Discussing sex, dating, and relationships can be a challenging topic for anyone, but it can be especially difficult for autistic teens who may struggle with social skills and communication. Teens on the spectrum oftentimes need explicit instruction on sex, especially when they tend to take things literally and do not always understand euphemisms. When talking about sex with your child, be very clear on the different parts of the body and their involvement, the act itself, how to be safe, the laws that address sexual conduct, romantic relationships, and morals and values. Help your teen to understand, be aware of, and appreciate their own body. It is important that you keep the conversation about sex ongoing. You might find that it is best to repeat information over time to help them understand and remember.

Here are 10 ways we can discuss and manage these issues with an autistic teen:

- Start early: Begin discussing sex and relationships early on in development, using age-appropriate language and concepts. Help your child understand their body parts while they are still young, and gradually add to the discussion as they get older. Try to keep things appropriate to their age and developmental levels.
- Use visual aids: Social stories, picture schedules, and cue cards can help autistic teens understand anatomy and sexual and relationship norms and expectations. These aids can be used to teach your child what is appropriate, where, and when.

- Provide accurate information: Give your teen factual and accurate information about sex, relationships, and consent. Talking about sex might be awkward for you and your child, but it is necessary. Let your child know that they are free to ask questions, and be open about answering. Teens typically talk about sex among themselves, and this can lead to misconceptions. The media also portrays unrealistic events and expectations. Find out what your child knows, and ensure that their information is accurate. While it is important to be open with your teen, you can also teach them that some things are private.

- Focus on personal safety: Discuss ways to stay safe in romantic and sexual situations, such as practicing safe sex and setting boundaries. Teach your teen the difference between healthy and unhealthy attraction, and help them to understand what behaviors are appropriate. You can work with your teen on practicing what to do and how to get help if they feel unsafe in a sexual or romantic relationship or situation. It is also important that you teach your child how to use the internet safely in regards to engaging in sexual discussion, exploration, or play online or over the phone.

- Model healthy relationships: Provide examples of positive relationship behaviors, and model how to maintain healthy, respectful relationships. Teach your child your values about sex and help them to understand the morals involved along with the physical acts.

- Encourage open communication: Help your teen to communicate their feelings and concerns about relationships and sexuality in a safe and supportive environment. Time, place, and appropriateness are important things to teach your teen. Talk with your teen about when it is appropriate to touch themselves and others. Help them understand who can touch them, where, and when. Be sure to use the actual terms for anatomy and acts instead of euphemisms.

- Teach social skills: Social skills such as active listening, empathy, and communication are essential for building healthy relationships. These are things your teen may struggle with, and so will need explicit instruction. Help your child to understand it is okay to say no, and to leave when they are uncomfortable. Teach them that engaging in sexual play is a choice, and they should not give in to pressure and do things that they do not want to do.

- Provide support and guidance: Offer your support and guidance for navigating romantic and sexual situations, such as discussing dating etiquette or providing guidance on interpreting social cues. Try to avoid using threats and scare tactics to control your teen's sex life. Instead, be open, honest, and clear, even when letting them know the risks involved with different sexual acts.

- Address specific concerns: Talk with your teen about specific concerns that may be unique to them, such as sensory sensitivities or anxiety related to romantic situations. Obsessive behaviors, routines and repetition can and will affect your teen's sex life, so be sure to talk with them about it. Some of the medications that your teen takes can also affect their sex lives. Due to developmental delays, your adult or young adult may display sexual behaviors that are typically attributed to teens. Be sure to talk to them about what is appropriate and inappropriate.

CHAPTER 5

LEARNING AND GROWING

I have no special talent. I am only passionately curious.
–Albert Einstein

AUTISM AND EDUCATION WITH DR. HANNON

Dr. LaChan Hannon and I spoke about the education system in relation to children with autism.

> I think we have to be intentional about how we train and prepare people, because this whole idea of, oh, I'm, you know, we're preparing people to teach all students. That is a lie.
>
> We're not preparing teachers to prepare to teach all students. We're preparing teachers to teach most students, right? We're not teaching them how to pay attention to the most vulnerable, recognizing that if you pay attention to the most vulnerable, everybody else is going to get what they need. And so part of the training that I do with teachers is 'I don't want you to just think about the student who's doing the best', right?... How you can encourage them—because you do

need to think about them. But who is the student that you're having the most difficulty working with or the parent you're having the most difficulty engaging? And how can we take what can work for them and scale up?

She added that teachers really need to love the kids.

You can't do the job of helping other people without love. And so you gotta put people in front of people. You have to have good, solid training and be willing to take the risk. And you have to love people. I'm not saying you're gonna like everybody, because I'm pretty sure I've had some students who certainly did not like me and that's fine. But you do have to love people, right? If you don't like kids, this ain't the job for you. I don't care how long you wanted to be a teacher; if you don't like people, you might need to be in a job where you don't have to talk to people.

HELPING YOUR TEEN THROUGH SCHOOL

Navigating the education system can be difficult for individuals with ASD. There are many ways you can help your teen as they go through school. I have already spoken about using visual aids, establishing routines, and helping your child with transitions.

You can also help your child understand their strengths and spend more time encouraging these than worrying about weaknesses. Sadly, when it comes to people with special needs, the focus is often on what they cannot do. This leads to low expectations from others, and self-doubt and low self-esteem within those with special needs. It is very important that you help your child identify and utilize their strengths. Learning what they are good at will help them become happier and more successful. It will lessen the time spent trying to accomplish frustrating tasks and help focus their attention and shape their goals.

The SWOT (Strengths, Weaknesses, Opportunities, and Threats) analysis is a useful tool that you can use with your child. Using this tool will help your child pinpoint the things they are good at and enjoy, along with areas for improvement. You can then help them to think about ways they can continue to grow, excel, and be productive, and things that may affect their growth. The SWOT analysis can be used to set goals with your child, identify possible challenges, and set strategies in place to overcome them.

Another strategy that you can use to help your child do well in school is task analysis. This involves breaking tasks into smaller, manageable pieces and then "chaining" these tasks until the overall goal is met. Your child may feel intimidated when faced with assignments and projects, and using the task analysis strategy will help them feel more confident and successful in their academic work. Showing them how to do task analysis will also help them become more independent as they apply the strategy themselves.

The first step is identifying what you want your child to know, and then finding out what knowledge they already have that is related to what you are going to teach them. Next is breaking down the task. You can ask someone to review how you compartmentalize what needs to be done to ensure that it makes sense. Afterwards, consider how you will teach your child—what visual aids, stories, modeling, technology, and so on will you use? Once you are ready, you can begin helping your child learn the skill, while taking notes on what works, what does not, and how to move forward.

One thing I cannot stress enough is the importance of developing a strong partnership with educators and school staff. Communication between parents and educators is key to ensuring that children with autism receive the support they need to succeed in school. Meet with the school to find out the programs they have and the accommodations they make for children with ASD. Ensure that you have an open, honest conversation with your child's teachers. You can ask how experienced they are in interacting with children with autism and share relevant information about your child. Let the teacher know your child's needs, habits, and interests, and talk about your concerns and expectations.

The lines of communication should be kept open beyond the initial meeting. Create a communication plan, stating how often you will meet with the teacher to discuss your child's progress and adjustments that need to be made. You can work with your child's teachers to create a daily, weekly, bi-weekly, etc. communication log where they write notes about your child in a journal that you can read and respond to. Maintaining communication with your child's teachers helps to ensure that you are both on the same page. This lessens confusion and reinforces lessons for your child as they receive similar information at home and at school.

While you know your child and want what is best for them, there are moments when you need to step back, trust your child's teacher, and allow them to do their jobs. Try to be open to suggestions and willing to explore new options to help your child. Sometimes your child's teacher may tell you something that may be hard to hear, but that you need to know and address or accept. Rather than immediately becoming defensive, listen, review the facts, observe your child, and then make a decision. However, be sure to maintain your boundaries. If there is something you feel uncomfortable with, and there are lines you do not want to cross, let the teachers know.

Another thing you can discuss with your child's teacher are ways to create a sensory-friendly environment, as this will help reduce distractions and improve focus. As I mentioned earlier, some schools have accommodations in place, and you can talk with them to find out more and come up with adjustments specific to your child. In addition, if your child struggles with verbal communication, then visual aids or assistive technology can help them participate more fully in the classroom. Examples include sign language, gestures, visual boards, picture exchange communication, and electronic devices.

Positive reinforcement, such as praise or rewards, can be a powerful tool for motivating children with autism and encouraging positive behavior. Positive reinforcement begins by looking at what causes the behavior, observing the behavior itself, and examining the consequences of the behavior.

You can use this strategy by first identifying a behavior that you want your child to adopt or improve. Then, choose how you will respond when your child acts a certain way. This response could be anything from saying "You did a good job, I am proud of you" to giving them treats, taking them out somewhere, or doing a fun activity with them. These types of responses are positive reinforcements. There are also negative reinforcements. It should be noted that negative reinforcement is in no way a punishment: It involves taking away something that causes your child to react a certain way. For example, you can remove something that makes your child uncomfortable. Once that thing is taken away, your child relaxes.

When using reinforcements, keep an eye on your child's progress. Note what works and what does not. Your responses may need adjustments, and your child's behavior will not magically change overnight. However, with patience and flexibility, you can help your child develop habits that will aid them in navigating life at school.

Do not be afraid to seek out additional resources and support. There are a variety of resources and supports available for children with autism and their families, including support groups, advocacy organizations, and professional services such as occupational therapy or speech therapy.

THE POWER OF LABELS

In an interview I had with the founder of Color of Autism, Camille Proctor, she urged parents to be their children's greatest champions. We spoke about the challenges children may face if their special needs are not acknowledged and accommodated.

> If we become stronger advocates for our children and stop denying who they are, and start to really build a community that embraces these people, [including] the police, then we can start dealing with some of the

systemic issues. But you see, when you have parents saying stuff like 'I don't want my son to have a label'...

All right, fine. Cool. No worries. Then he'll get 89418. What's that? His prison inmate number. And they're like what do you mean? She added. 'Cause you don't want him to have a label, so the school said 'Oh, he's oppositional defiant'. You think that's a good term? So basically, you've just labeled your child bad, so you fed into the system of your child being a throw-away kid. He's bad. So you're just fast-tracking him into the prison system, right? The criminal justice system, because you don't wanna have a label.

Ohh, don't wanna have an IEP. Don't worry, he doesn't need an individual education plan because you don't like the way that sounds. I said, but there's a little white kid in Harvard. He has an IEP in college and you know what? He's probably gonna get a Ph.D. with it while yours sits in your basement playing Game Boy or whatever, you know. Fine. You don't need to make anybody's life better that's related to you and has your DNA. And they look at me 'cause, you know, I'm to the point where I don't coddle people because the reality of it is that Black people have never been coddled. And even when we do get coddled, we don't understand how to effectively force the change. We can't see because we're too busy licking our wounds.

ACADEMIC CHALLENGES FOR BLACK AND BROWN TEENS

Studies have shown that children who are white and from a higher socioeconomic background are more likely to be recognized to have been diagnosed with ASD than those who are Asian, Black, Latinx, and from low socioeconomic backgrounds. In fact, white children were 19% more likely to be diagnosed with ASD than Black children, and 65% more than Latinx children. Kids from Black communities often experience a delay of 3-5 years after concerns have been voiced before receiving a diagnosis. As a result, children from low socioeconomic communities and Asian, Black, and Latinx groups often miss out on accommodations, interventions, and medical assistance. Factors that affect the rate of diagnosis include access to healthcare, geographical location, racism, discrimination, and lack of knowledge and information about ASD and other special needs (Alyward et al., 2021).

Many Black and Brown parents experience difficulty getting evaluations and aid. Racial and ethnic minorities with ASD have been found to have decreased access to treatment services because of language and logistic barriers (e.g., transportation, childcare, and job accommodations), as well as a lack of knowledge of existing services. Black and Brown caregivers have also reported multiple service rejections for reasons unknown to them. Another challenge is a lack of programs and/or educators trained to help their children. Some parents are treated with disrespect from healthcare professionals and have their concerns about their child tossed aside. Pearson and Meadan (2018) noted that 9 out of 11 Black mothers in their study had to advocate for their children with ASD to access services.

Teens from minority and lower-income homes tend to have less access to education and jobs, leading to challenges in life after high school. Programs created for families with a higher socioeconomic status often fail to adequately meet the needs of minorities. Assistance and interventions for people with ASD are also not always present in struggling communities. Black and Brown teens also experienced more difficulties in social interactions, living independently, developing adaptive behaviors, and practicing self-care (Shattuck et al., 2019).

ATTENDING SCHOOL WITH DR. DURR

While speaking with Dr. Angel Durr, I also asked her about executive functioning challenges she may have had in school.

> I had great teachers along the way that were willing to work with me and take the extra time to help me where I had issues with that kind of thing. Like, for example, one of the things that stands out is my teacher in Math. I wouldn't sit still in class and pay attention to what I needed to do, so he actually let me play my Game Boy in the class and I would pay attention and I would know what I was supposed to be doing and I'd be able to follow directions.
>
> When I was not occupied and I was just sitting there bored, I would have a really hard time doing what I was supposed to be doing in the way that I was supposed to be doing it—so teachers would make accommodations for me. [They] let me redo assignments after class as many times as I needed to so I could follow the directions, because sometimes I would do an assignment really fast and not follow the directions properly, and the teacher would be like— hey, I think you just did this too fast. And they'd let me redo it. And then I also got into a lot of extracurricular activities.
>
> But then some things like driving were really hard. I just ended up not driving 'til I was 19, and that was unfortunate because I was behind a lot of my peers.

She explained that passing the driver's test was a major challenge.

I just wasn't there yet, and it took me a little bit longer, but I passed by the skin of my teeth, and then I just spent the time after that doing what I needed to do and practicing as much as possible. I just took a little longer to do things. And I'm grateful that I had people that were willing to wait for me to do things in my own time instead of rushing me 'cause a lot of it wasn't that I couldn't, I just needed more time to process it all. Because I was processing, my brain was processing so much already and that was just one more thing that I had to process.

She also mentioned that she had sleep and dietary issues.

I didn't sleep. I started taking melatonin at a young age because I had such a hard time sleeping dietary-wise. Yeah, I would eat the same foods and my mom would just get mad that I wouldn't ever want to eat anything else. But I like these few things, like cereal was definitely one of my staples. I constantly ate cereal—the same cereal all the time. It would become frustrating sometimes if something I liked wasn't available. I just wouldn't eat. And my mom would get really mad at me about that kind of stuff.

But, I mean, I was a teenager, so if there was something I wanted, I would just go get it. Like I started working at 16 specifically so that I could buy the food that I wanted and have my own disposable income for that kind of stuff because it was frustrating. I wanted very specific things, and if I didn't have them, I would just go without eating entirely and then sleeping. I went a lot of times where I wouldn't sleep really well during the week. I would sleep all weekend really, so I would just kind of do what I needed to do to get caught up on things in my own time.

Everything was just about me doing things in my own time and keeping myself busy. The more I kept myself busy, the easier it was.

HELPING YOUR TEEN PRACTICE SELF-CARE

When talking to your teen about self-care, let them know that it does not mean changing themselves. Self-care is a normal and important part of life, and it is in no way selfish. Taking care of yourself ensures that you are healthy and able to perform well at home, school, and all other aspects of life. Your mental and physical well-being is something that should be given priority. Self-care encompasses getting adequate rest, eating healthy, following proper medical protocols, caring for your mental, emotional, and social needs, and more.

Teaching your child how to practice self-care helps them to become happy, independent, and productive people. Self-care starts with you. Being an effective parent sometimes means stopping and taking time for yourself. In my conversations with parents who have children on the spectrum, they all say getting in time for myself is extremely important to the health and well-being of the whole family. An analogy of this would be when you are flying on the plane, the attendants give the safety talk and tell you to put on your oxygen mask first before you put on the child's. As a mother, you may feel compelled to take care of your child and neglect yourself. But in the long run—if you don't get oxygen and you die—how can you help your child? Self-care for you is important.

Pio Ferro is a Cuban American with a 23-year-old son with ASD. He told me that his son Tony functions around the age of a four-year-old.

"We know that he was going to be literally our baby for the rest of his life. For the rest of our life."

I asked if finding services for their son is getting progressively more difficult now that he is considered an adult.

He said he's lived in Florida, Texas and New Jersey. And out of all the places he's lived New Jersey has been the best in terms of finding services. He says the state has made it possible to put his son in high school an additional year. And Tony looks forward to going. He says if left up to his son, he would just stay home and eat snacks all day. Activity with others outside of home helps keep Tony and the rest of the family healthy. Ferro notes that because of the high level of need for their son, it's important that he and his wife find time to spend with each other, spend time alone and time with their other two girls who are not diagnosed with ASD. His advice for parents facing challenges like his is to make time for yourself.

"Try to find somebody that can take care of your child that you trust so you can get out and go to a movie. And you know, go to your favorite restaurant. Go have ice cream. Go to the gym."

Self-care helps to relieve you of stress and frustration, and improves your communication with your family. It also serves as a way of modeling self-care for your teen. They will be more likely to pick up the self-care habits they see you exhibiting, especially when they observe the positive effects of doing these things. Practice emotional awareness as well. Talk to your teen about noticing when you are feeling anxious and what you do to calm yourself. In engaging in self-care as a family, you help to build a stronger bond among the members.

You can also check in with each other as a family. Set aside time to share and talk about your day, hopes, dreams, fears, setbacks, and achievements. Provide a warm and supportive environment for everyone to share, and show your love and support towards each member. You can talk to your teen about moments when they are happiest and most comfortable. In your daily conversations, try to help them to find and discuss the bright points of their day. Give them space to think and share their thoughts. Work with your teen to find out stressors in their life, and how they can cope with them. In discussing the highs and lows of their day, you can help them to practice self-reflection.

Another aspect of self-care is loving and accepting yourself. Help your teen to practice gratitude, appreciate their strengths, and acknowledge their worth. Their needs are just as important as anyone else's, and they are valued and loved. Self-care can be scheduled into your teen's day, and you can create routines for them to follow. The use of social stories and video aids will help them understand and adapt self-care behaviors. Establishing goals and finding a purpose is also a part of self-care. It helps to motivate individuals and gives them direction along with a sense of accomplishment. Talk to your teen about their dreams and work with them to create and accomplish goals at home, school, and in their social lives.

Practicing self-care does not have to cost a lot of money. There are a lot of things you can do at home. You can engage your teen in doing a hobby, running a bath, going for a walk, spending time in nature, meditating, and exercising. Other self-care activities include listening to music, watching a movie, and socializing with close family and friends. You can develop new hobbies and try your hand at learning new things. Ask your teen some things they would like to do, and make time to do it with them, or allow them to do them on their own if feasible.

Autistic teenagers have a range of medical needs, which may include behavioral therapy, speech therapy, and medication management. Additionally, they may have co-occurring conditions, such as anxiety or ADHD, that require specific medical attention.

Medication

Contact your healthcare professional to discuss whether your child should be given medication. Your doctor will extensively review your child's history before making a recommendation. People with ASD may be placed on medication if their symptoms negatively affect their ability to function effectively at home, school, and in the wider community. Each individual responds to medication differently, and the type of medication and dosage may need several adjustments until a balance can be found. The side effects of medications are also something your doctor will discuss with you.

Here are some medications approved by the Food and Drug Administration (FDA) that your doctor may prescribe:

- Risperidone (Risperdal): This is an atypical antipsychotic used to treat self-injury, aggression, and tantrums in autistic children aged 5 to 16 years old.
- Atomoxetine (Strattera), guanfacine (Tenex), and methylphenidate (Ritalin): These are stimulant medications used to treat symptoms of hyperactivity and inattention.
- Anti-anxiety medications
- Amitriptyline (Elavil), desipramine (Norpramin), and clomipramine (Anafranil): These are called tricyclics and are antidepressants for obsessive-compulsive behaviors and depression.
- Fluoxetine (Prozac) and sertraline (Zoloft): Known as Selective Serotonin Reuptake Inhibitors (SSRIs), these are antidepressants used to treat symptoms caused by chemical imbalances in the body. SSRIs are used to reduce repetitive and aggressive behaviors, and anxiety.
- Carbamazepine (Tegretol), clonazepam (Klonopin), and diazepam (Valium): These are anticonvulsants that are used to treat seizures

While I have no experience with the medications listed above, research shows that they are the ones most commonly prescribed by medical professionals for individuals with ASD.

Getting your child to take their medications is not always easy. Some taste terrible, and as your child gets older, they may refuse to take the medicine because they do not like the side effects. Most parents crush the pills and disguise them in food and drink when their children are younger. This works for some, but not everyone. For one thing, the combination of pills and food may taste horrible, and your child may begin acting out when it is time for them to eat their medicine-enhanced meal. If your child takes a long time to drink their juice, then the dosage may not work properly, and medicine may settle at the bottom of the cup. Sneaking medication into their food also means that they do not explicitly learn the importance of taking their medication, how much to take, and when to take it. As a result, many healthcare professionals recommend teaching your child to swallow the pills.

Children with ASD may also struggle to take medications due to sensory challenges. The smell, taste, and texture can prove challenging for them. Some cannot easily swallow pills due to difficulties with their coordination and motor skills. They may be able to push it towards their throat with their tongue, but their swallow reflex may not activate, leading to them choking. Another reason why your child may struggle to take medication is because of anxiety, fear of needles, and fear of the medication itself.

You can tell if your child is ready to swallow pills if they are able to eat foods such as oatmeals or applesauce, as these tend to have chunks along with the liquid. Practice having them gulp water then eating something small like rice, a bean, or a piece of pasta. You can model doing so yourself, then encourage them to try. As they master the task, slowly increase the size of the food item they are swallowing until it is pill-sized. You can also try having your child swallow the pill along with their favorite juice.

When giving your child medicine, use lots of modeling and positive reinforcement. Make sure they understand the importance of taking their medication. You can add it to their routine and use alarms to remind them when it is time to take another dose. Pictures, videos, and social stories can also be used. Be gentle but firm in reminding your teen to take their medication. If they have objections and concerns, listen to them patiently, answer their questions, and discuss possible ways forward. You can involve your healthcare provider in the discussion with your teen to ensure that your child feels heard and that they receive clear and accurate information and instructions. You may be tempted to hover, but at some point you may have to step back and allow your teen to take their medications on their own. Help them to understand that this is a part of their self-care and helps them in their daily lives.

Teen Care and Therapy

Cognitive, behavioral, play, speech, and other forms of therapy are a regular part of treatment programs for individuals with ASD.

Choosing the right therapist for your child and your family is very important and influences the effectiveness of the treatment. When selecting a therapist, you can gain recommendations for your main healthcare professional, your child's school, or trusted ASD organizations and groups. Be sure to do a lot of research to learn about the different types of therapists and the services they provide. The experience of the therapist is also something to consider. They may be well-recommended, but are they familiar with working with children with ASD?

If the therapist offers consultations, you can use that opportunity to get to know them to see if they are someone you would be interested in working with. Other important things to find out is if they are licensed and insured. Their personality, how well they get along with your teen, and their location are also factors to consider. It is also okay to change therapists if you see the need to do so. Your child deserves someone who they are comfortable with and who brings out the best in them, and you should never settle for anything less.

With teens, it is not always easy to figure out what behavior is a part of them growing up and being hormonal, and what behavior is something that needs to be addressed through therapy. Some signs to look for are persistent anxiety and depression, suicidal thoughts and attempts, self-harm, and persistent self-isolation. Your child may experience sudden changes in behavior, such as changes in friend groups, lowered academic performance, or changes in habits and in appearance—for example, dramatic weight loss or gain, hair loss, or constantly looking drained.

Suggesting therapy may not go over well with your teen. When introducing the topic to them, do so in a calm, loving environment. Talk about what you have observed about them, your concerns, and why going to therapy is a needed solution. If your teen becomes angry and defensive, be patient and hear them out. You can involve them in the therapy selection process and reassure them that you will respect their privacy, and that the therapist is bound by confidentiality laws.

TEEN CARE WITH JANET JONES-JORDAN

In my interview with Janet Jones-Jordan, she mentioned how parents should be vigilant about establishing in the IEP at school that their child get help with executive functioning skills. And the parent needs to work directly with their child at home.

> Teachers have a responsibility and a role to help students understand what the components of some of those tough management skills are, and they need to practice with the students to help them develop those executive functioning skills.

She noted flexible thinking, working memory, self-monitoring, planning, and prioritizing. She said children, even those who are not on the spectrum, struggle with tasks like these.

> It should be part of the training that they receive at the school.

Jones added with her son and other teens on the spectrum, personal hygiene is an issue. Something as simple as shoes can be a big challenge for some students with autism or intellectual disability.

> And so, parents should be doing and practicing these skills at home. Don't just expect the school to work with your child. You need to be practicing these skills at home also to help your teen be successful. I have posters that I will put at home, you know, that kind of gives things as simple as washing your hands. [It will say] Get your hands wet. Pump 3 pumps of soap. Rub your hands for 20 seconds. You know, all of those things that are important for him to remember in case he forgets. He can look over at the poster.

She also has one near his bed.

> You know, those type of things that's gonna help them because ultimately—and the sad part is—we're not going to always be here for our children, and I think as a parent of a child with special needs, one of our greatest fears is 'What's gonna happen to my child when I'm no longer here?' Those are things you need to be thinking about. Those are things that you need to be preparing for.

CHAPTER 6

STAYING SAFE

To all those mothers and fathers who are struggling with teenagers, I say, just be patient: Even though it looks like you can't do anything right for a number of years, parents become popular again when kids reach 20.
–Marian Wright Edelman

Content warning: the following chapter contains true stories about violence against teens and adults with autism.

THE SAFETY TALK

Janet Jones-Jordan—and other parents of Black and Brown children with autism—says that "THE TALK" or safety conversation Black parents often have with children about what to do if stopped by a police officer is an ongoing process, one that evolves and is often complicated.

> So my son. My son is my passion, and Jeremiah was not diagnosed until he was six years old, and prior to his diagnosis, I experienced many barriers to even getting to a diagnosis. He was being tested for everything but autism.

I know that he doesn't understand that safety is an issue for Black men in this country. I also have an older son who would be 30 next month, and I've had what we call the talk with him. I've also had that talk with my younger son, Jeremiah. Jeremiah is what we call a wanderer… He will run or he will, you know, flee. And for that reason alone, I never allow my younger son to ride along in the car with my older son for fear that if my older son is stopped for whatever reason, the blaring lights, the sirens, all of those things, may terrify my younger son and he may start running. I think that in my family we have a little of an advantage that some families don't have. My son's father is a police officer. My brother is a police officer, but again, it doesn't negate the fact that if something happens, Jeremiah may run because he's afraid.

A study by the Ruderman Foundation found that "people with disabilities are more likely to be unjustly harmed by law enforcement." Researchers added in that report "it is safe to say that a third to a half of all use-of force incidents involve a disabled civilian" (Perry & Carter-Long, 2016 p. 5, 7).

"As of June 2021, the Legislative Analysis and Public Policy Association reported that 25 states have laws or programs that address mental health emergencies" (Hill & Widgery, 2022, p.10)—or ways to keep police from having to respond. One of them was passed in Illinois because of Stephon Watts, a 15-year-old Black autistic youth. Calumet police shot and killed him inside his home after he had a meltdown in 2012.

Camille Proctor explained what happened:

So the family plan, which they worked out with the hospital and the police, was that if Stephon got to a point where they couldn't handle him, they would call the police and the police would take him to the

> hospital. This particular day… he… things escalated. But then they de-escalated. So, when the cop came to the house, the dad said it's ok, it's fine, it's fine, it's fine. Well, the cop pushed the dad, who was very weak, out of the way. And they ran in the house. Stephon got scared and he ran to the basement. So, when he ran to the basement, all the parents heard was pow, pow, pow, pow, pow! And he was dead. The cops said that Stephon pulled a knife on him. But it was in fact a butter knife.

She questions why other means couldn't have been used to de-escalate the situation. The Chicago Tribune (2012) reports officers had been called "to subdue Stephon 10 times in less than two years, using tasers at least once."

> I tell parents, stop calling the police on your kids. Like the aggressive behavior does not happen overnight. And I'm not blaming the parents at all, because we do the best that we can. But the aggressive behavior does not happen overnight. And when you see it escalating, you gotta figure out ways to de-escalate and create interventions to make that person feel comfortable enough so that they can calm down. But first and foremost, there just needs to be more understanding, more information a little more widely disseminated within communities of color so that we can do better in protecting them against police brutality or police murders. I mean, honestly, that's what it is. That's what happened to Stephon. He was murdered in his own home.

She added that there needs to be better training so that Black and Brown people on the autism spectrum aren't targeted with aggression.

When people go, police training! Yeah, they do need to be trained but it's not a two hour lunch and learn. You know, you can't give them a couple of donuts and some coffee and say okay, now—off you go.

Stephon's sister Renee' Watts told me she didn't want to relive the traumatic story in an interview but allowed me to share part of the talk she had with the advocacy group Disability Lead in 2021. Ms. Watts stated the following:

Instead of getting officers with compassion, life experience, or patience, my father was met with two overworked, stressed out, hostile police officers who were tired of dealing with Stephon. In the aftermath of the shooting, the police chief of Calumet City said that Stephon had made poor decisions.

But anyone who understands the dynamics of autism spectrum disorder knows communication and decision making are some of the challenges with the neurological disorder. Stephon Watts' family lobbied the state of Illinois to adopt a new law called the Community Emergency Services and Support Act, or CESSA. The new law, also called the Stephon Watts Act, prohibits police officers from responding to mental health or medical emergencies.

TEACHING YOUR CHILD HOW TO BE SAFE

Safety can be a concern for autistic teens due to a variety of factors, including difficulties with social communication, sensory sensitivities, and executive functioning challenges. It really depends on your specific teen's needs. We need to create plans to address safety concerns related to wandering, online safety, sensory sensitivities, and other issues that may affect autistic teens. It is important to work with healthcare providers, educators, and other professionals to develop individualized safety plans and strategies that meet the unique needs of each individual. Things like teaching social boundaries, addressing your child's sensory sensitivities, and encouraging community involvement can help keep your child safe. The following are some more steps you can take.

Developing a Safety Plan

Create a personalized safety plan that addresses the specific needs and concerns of the individual. This plan can include identifying safe places to go in an emergency, establishing a communication plan, and teaching safety skills such as road safety. Be sure to list out all the relevant people such as family members, school staff, healthcare professionals, caretakers, and neighbors. You can help keep your child safe by making sure that the people listed are aware of your child's diagnosis and needs. This helps them to be prepared when interacting with the child, and to take action when they notice anything amiss. Ask your teen to always carry identification, including a contact number. Safety plans can also be included in your child's IEP.

Teaching Self-Advocacy Skills

Help your teen learn to advocate for their own safety needs, such as communicating with a trusted adult or setting boundaries with others. It is not always easy determining who to tell about an ASD diagnosis and when to tell them. Not everyone will react with love and support when finding out that someone is autistic, and that can be emotionally and mentally damaging to teens. On the other hand, your teen may feel as if they are hiding an important part of themselves if they do not disclose their disorder. You can let your teen know that self-disclosure is their choice, and prepare them for how people might respond. Help them understand that negative reactions are more a reflection on the person reacting than it is on them.

Tell your teen that having autism is a part of who they are, but it is not their entire identity. Encourage them to learn more about ASD, and connect them with groups that are there to help and support them. You can engage your teen in self-reflection, so they are able to identify their habits and needs and come up with strategies to address any challenges where needed. Teach your child to stand up for themselves while being calm and respectful. While you are there for them, they can also take charge and advocate for themselves.

Self-advocacy is especially important when it comes to sexual activities. As your child may struggle with understanding the emotions and behavior of others, they may not realize when they are being approached inappropriately. Teach your child about physical space and boundaries. There are some things that are okay and some that are not, and some things that close family members are allowed to do that others should never try. Work with your child to ensure that they can recognize and leave dangerous situations, and that they know how to ask for help.

Teaching Stranger Safety

Show your teen how to recognize and respond to potentially dangerous situations, such as interacting with strangers or accepting rides from unfamiliar people. Rather than teaching your child to never talk to strangers, teach them how to recognize whom they can approach for help and whom they should avoid. You can use pictures to show them how public safety officials such as firemen and policemen are dressed and where they usually can be found. Let your child know that they should never let anyone separate them from a group and lead them away. Gifts and food should not be accepted from strangers, and they should be wary of random people trying to hug them or take their hand.

Teaching Technology Safety

Teach the teen how to use technology safely, including online safety and appropriate use of social media. Let them know to never give out the personal information online nor agree to meet up with strangers. If someone is bothering them, they should block and report that person. Work with your teen to identify sites and apps that are safe versus those that are not. I have parental trackers on my son's phone. I periodically check online history on his laptop and school computer. There are many tech-tools you can use that will help you keep your child safe.

Teaching Emergency Procedures

Teach your teen how to respond to emergencies, such as calling 911, evacuating a building, and using a fire extinguisher.

AUTISM AND THE POLICE WITH DR. ONAIWU AND MS. PROCTOR

Dr. Morénike Giwa Onaiwu is a Black woman diagnosed with autism who works with the non-profit organization Advocacy Without Borders. She says, although some states or cities have similar legislation, it's not on a national scale.

The National Council of State Legislators reports that "since September, 2019 at least 13 states have Medicaid-funded mobile crisis teams (Hill & Widgery, 2022, p.14)" But Ball and Jeffery-Wilensky (2020) of Spectrum News reports laws on the books requiring police to have training to ensure that autistic people are safe when they encounter an officer is not a national standard.

So, Giwa Oainwu takes extra precautions to keep herself safe. She has five children ages 20, 19, 18, 14, and 12. One of her adult sons has low support autism, or Asperger's. She says she often role-plays with him, telling him if approached by an officer to refrain from showing any behaviors that might make the officer nervous.

During our interview, Dr. Onaiwu recalled how police encounters don't always have to be bad ones.

> So my younger children did a lot of wandering and
> so we have, you know, locked some of the doors and

had baby gates and alarms. But, you know, sometimes they were fast. And so, there was an incident where my daughter learned how to unstrap herself out of the stroller and disappeared.

I'm literally pushing her, but the reason I didn't feel her get up is because I also had a baby bag hanging on the back of the stroller, which gave it weight. I could have felt the weight—the difference, you know. And so, she got up. She disappeared.

We're at church, you know. Every way I'm freaking out. She doesn't really answer her name or anything like that. So I'm in tears trying to figure out what's going on, looking all around frantically. And there happened to be a man who wasn't working. It was his day off, but he was a police officer. And so when he noticed my distress, he asked what was going on, and asked for a picture of my daughter because the rest of us were frantic and running around and not probably doing the right thing.

I guess with his training… you know… he might as well have been Superman as far as I was concerned. Like I was so teary-eyed and overwhelmed and grateful, you know, and thanking him for it. And she wasn't scared. He got her to come to him.

He approached her in a way that didn't set her off or make her frightened. You know, it was just a huge blessing. And he did this not seeking any recognition or reward or anything. I didn't even get a chance to get his name to thank him when this happened. And so that was a wonderful experience.

But she also shared a police encounter that was quite alarming while driving slowly on the road because she was tired that day.

> I was stopped and the person, you know, started asking me questions and when I'm nervous, you know, or when I'm trying to focus or concentrate, I engage in echolalia. I might not even know that I'm doing it and so because unfortunately, I'm an adult, he thought I was mocking him.

She explained that when the officer spoke to her in a southern twang, she copied his tone.

> So he said something like, 'Where are you going, ma'am?' And I was like, 'Where are you going, ma'am?' And I didn't say it to be mean. I said it, even in the same tone that he said it. But that's just how I process. I don't... I couldn't figure out how to say it in my head. And he was like, 'What's your name?' And I like, pause for a second because I was like, oh, my gosh, I don't wanna repeat. I don't wanna say: What's your name again? Because then you think I'm being rude.
>
> So, I'm stopping myself from talking, so now I'm not answering so that he finds that weird. I'm not making eye contact. He finds that shifty. And so he says get out of the car and I get out and I have a stimming device. Like, you know, it's a little toy wire coiling thing that I use. And I have it in my hands. And so I'm using it to calm myself down. So I can try to address him, make eye contact. And he draws for his weapon.

Thankfully, she says the officer saw the fear in her eyes and allowed her to explain that the shiny metallic item was a stimming device she used to calm herself down.

But what if I hadn't been able to form speech properly? What if I had burst into tears? Or what if I continued to use echolalia? What if I had got scared and tried to drive off and pass him up, you know? Like anything could have happened like, you know, it's just... it's frightening. And he wasn't trying to be cruel or mean or discriminatory. He just didn't know what was happening. And as far as he was concerned, it was unknown, therefore potentially a threat.

Color of Autism founder Camille Proctor has conducted police training sessions for the autism community and says she found the process needs to be more than academic.

Camille Proctor

I think that it has to be organic and they have to actually care. So we had a program where we took teenagers such as my son, and we put them in a group with cops, sheriffs, different people from law enforcement, and they would meet on Saturdays just to talk about their special interests and likes and stuff like that. We did it like that because we wanted the cops to organically build these bonds with these kids and get to know them as human beings, not these theoretical things about how a person acts.

So, one good example I have is that I had one of the sheriffs in a place in North Carolina, he said, 'I walked up on this kid the other day and he was looking at this car and he was looking and looking. And I said, 'Do you like that license plate? And the little boy said yeah.

'And the reason I said that is because I remember your son likes license plates.' And he said 'so, we had a whole conversation about different license plates, historical.' And he said this conversation went on for about 15 minutes. And he said before that, if he was looking at a license plate, I would think rest assured, he was trying to break into that car or vandalize it.

He said but now I look at it in a totally different way, because that young man was looking at the license plate and he was flapping his hands. The sheriff said 'I remember your son too'. He kept referring to my son: 'I remember your son used to do that, he used to go woo woo woo! And so I knew what I was dealing with immediately. He said 'So I thank you for the opportunity for me to get to understand these young people better'. And so that's the type of things that I think are transformative in regards to teaching and educating a police force.

Dr. Morénike Giwa Onaiwu also says that she warns parents that introducing their child to a police officer is not always the best course of action.

Dr. Morenike Giwa Onaiwu

That stuff makes me upset when people say, 'Take your child to the police officer and introduce them to all the officers on duty and let them understand what they do and who your child is and what they look like and all that'. I think that's really well-intentioned, and I applaud the spirit behind that, but I think that in reality, that's not gonna work. First of all, so no one's ever gonna have a day off? [What about when the officers who know your child are not on duty?]

I think people give themselves a false sense of security. I do think that there is some benefit to doing that, like if your child is a, you know, a wanderer or elopes, sometimes you might not have an up-to-date picture.

You don't know what context this person has. Just because you're introducing your child, you don't know what their perspective is of people with certain disabilities. Do they see them as a danger or threat? Do they see them as out of control? So, you know, we're looking through the eyes of a parent with love. That's not the eyes they're looking through.

Although many autistic adults and advocates agree that police training should be standard across the country, it isn't. According to Ball & Jeffery-Wilensky (2020) of Spectrum News, the Riverside County Sheriff's Department in California has a mandatory 15 hour autism training requirement for their recruits. Being hired by the department results in a further 4 hours of training. But in other places, training could be a 15-minute video. Quality and quantity vary. That's why parents and those living on The Spectrum say they take added precautions.

SAFETY FOR TEENS WITH DR. DURR

In my interview with Dr. Angel Durr, we discussed safety for young teens and how to read a room, especially when something is dangerous. Statistics show that often people living on the spectrum are victims of crime. She explained the challenges with safety she faced as a teen and adult, and spoke about how her mom was murdered years ago.

"Safety is very important to me as an autistic person. Because we're not good at all about knowing when we're in safe situations or not. And that's one of the scariest parts of being on the Spectrum. And even though I joke and say it's not a death sentence— like for some of us, it's a possibility because we can put ourselves into dangerous situations very easily, unknowingly because we are naive to things. I was definitely 100 percent one of those people as a young person. And I'm actually grateful in that way though that I wasn't accepted into certain groups because if I would have been there was a potential that I could have gotten into a lot of dangerous situations.

"Even as an adult, there's times when I confront a situation and I feel uncomfortable. Now I just run away like—I will literally get up and leave and run off—people I've been on dates with. Because I've learned that in those situations it's best to just get out of the way and like leave, and there were times when I was young where people would be doing things and I would be there and I would realize like this is not what I want to be doing. But I would feel like the pressure to want to belong and I would do something that I had no business doing or hang around people that I shouldn't hang around."

She said now that she's older, reading situations can be even more frightening.

I feel like sometimes when you're older, it's actually a little scarier because people can come in with the intention of trying to make you think that they are, you know, somebody that you can trust and then do something to you. And that's pretty scary. It's even scarier to me now as an adult and so I don't tend to hang out with a lot of people I don't know and stuff like that.

My mom was walking alone by her apartment and was shot and found dead in the streets. I do feel like my mom's murder was a result of her Autism and lack of safety awareness. I myself have done a lot of things many would consider dangerous and she was living in the most dangerous part of Dallas.

AUTISM AND THE ROAD AHEAD

I spoke with several parents and advocates who shared how they empathized with Stephon Watts' family. Many parents like Lola Dada-Olley and her husband Tosan shared that there should be a national standard.

Lola Dada-Olley

> I think what is more important is to have as many police officers trained and just understanding that not all differences are visible. And sometimes when one is visible and one is not and some people are actually members of two traditionally oppressed groups – one can amplify the other.

Something perhaps like what U.S. Congresswoman Katie Porter from California proposed with the Mental Health Justice Act of 2022. This act provides funding to local communities so that trained health professionals can be placed in mental health response units and be dispatched for emergency calls.

The law was passed by the House in 2022 but failed in the Senate, preventing it from becoming federal law. That means across the country, mental health response units are sparsely scattered—partially due to lack of funding.

This training is essential as autistic individuals can become overwhelmed and react intensely in stressful situations. According to the National Autistic Society (2020), when stressed or scared, people on the spectrum may cry, shout, or try to escape a situation. They could also become aggressive and lash out toward others. Then there's the issue of understanding dangerous situations.

The federal Office for Victims of Crime (n.d.) reports that if you have a disability you are more than twice as likely to be a victim of a violent crime than those without one. In 2022, the Journal of Autism and Developmental Disorders reported that "almost 60 percent of autistic adults reported experiencing sexual violence and or physical violence. These rates were significantly higher than those reported by non-autistic adults," which stood around 28 percent (Gibbs et al., p. 6). Sexual harassment and domestic violence are some on the top of the list. And strangers aren't always the perpetrators; sometimes it's family and those considered friends. Angel Durr agrees that standard training for law enforcement is needed because it's important that victims don't become victimized by those who are supposed to protect them.

Dr. Angel Durr

> We need people that are better trained to understand the differences and distinctions, but we don't have them yet. And so it's important for us to, you know, be around people that we trust and take the proper precautions when necessary if we are going to do certain things. So that we are safe.

CHAPTER 7

EMPLOYMENT AND RESOURCES

The purpose of human life is to serve, and to show
compassion and the will to help others.
–Albert Schweitzer

JOB-HUNTING WITH ASD

Finding a job after high school can be a challenge for young adults
on the autism spectrum. One suggestion is to seek out Vocational
Rehabilitation Services. According to the ARC Autism Now (2011),
in 2009, 59 percent of people with ASD landed a job after receiving
VRS. That's pretty good. However, the agency also noted that another
study found that although it found 66 percent of youth with ASD
worked sometime after high school, "a few years later, only 47% of
these youth had jobs (ARC Autism Now, 2011, p.8)." This suggests
that getting a job may be possible but keeping it may also be an
added challenge.

Many resources suggest that you look for organizations who
partner with businesses who offer the autism community an inclusive
space. One of those organizations is The Adult Autism Center of
Lifetime Learning. However, there are sometimes local smaller
organizations that can also offer a helping hand.

Some autism moms that I've spoken with, like author Faith Clarke, who wrote "Parenting Like a Ninja: An Autism Mom's Guide to Professional Productivity" have been working in inclusivity for years. The educator and entrepreneur has been a K-12 teacher and taught on the college level. She says often parents of autistic adults create businesses that their children can work from home. It's often the only path to employment many ASD adults choose. But Clarke believes parents need to advocate more for being included rather than remain excluded from work and social spaces. In a recorded interview she shared the following:

> I have humans that don't fit in. I'm a human that doesn't fit into the typical environment. And then I have humans at home who don't fit in. And while I have the luxury of saying, OK, no worries, we'll build a business, and you will earn money through our business. Every parent of a child with autism or neuro variance should not have to start a business to provide their child with meaningful work.

She added that the inclusivity that most of the world is talking about in business and society needs to start with community and individuals that actually care about each other. And that means that if people in your community really begin to "know you and your child individually" understanding where they thrive and what they can contribute to the community, inclusivity becomes a whole lot easier.

Take for example this fictional woman we'll call Amanda:

Having been diagnosed with autism as a child, Amanda grew up with lots of support from her parents and teachers. However, entering the working world proved to be quite difficult for her. During interviews, Amanda struggled to make eye contact, had difficulty communicating, and sometimes engaged in echolalia. Amanda often left her interviews knowing she would not get the job. She was knowledgeable in her area and had a detailed portfolio and good references but struggled to sell herself. The companies she applied to seemed to be more focused on her lack of interpersonal skills than on her qualifications.

I believe Amanda is struggling to fit into a system that sees her as an outlier. So the added stress of not being herself and pushing against her difference is something she really shouldn't have to endure. If the "community" or business she was trying to join was really inclusive and didn't see her differences as negative attributes, then all of the internal stress she experienced would likely not be as intense. But many would argue that business or workplace settings are not family settings, so there are expectations employees need to meet. But I would also argue that expectations of people in the workplace change. What was "acceptable" for a man or woman working in the 1950s is not the same as in 2023. Add ethnicity into the mix, and you can see even bigger changes in expectations.

Another issue that our fictional Amanda might also struggle with is self-disclosure. There is always the question of whether she should talk about her autism during interviews or if she should speak up once she's been hired. Some companies might ask about her disability on the application. Amanda's internal dialogue might go something like this:

> "What if they did not hire me because of my diagnosis? It's supposed to be illegal but, you know, people still do it. Or what if I was just a pity hire? Sure, I would have a job, but would they treat me as some sort of mascot or something?
>
> "Knowing when to talk about having ASD is hard. I have a lot of skills and knowledge, but sometimes I need support, and some environments can be challenging."

Here is a possible experience Amanda might face after being assured by employers that accommodations would be made for her needs:

> "It basically amounted to them telling (everyone) about my ASD and asking them to be aware of it. It

was really uncomfortable, I didn't, you know, want my business out there like that. Some of my colleagues were nice, and some tried to be but came off as being really condescending. I had a co-worker who was mad because she felt I was getting preferential treatment due to my autism. But I wasn't...you know, all my employers did was tell people."

While Amanda might enjoy her work, the environment may not be one that is the right fit for her. However, she may find it very hard to leave. She may think something like the following:

"I would basically be back to square one. Back to interviewing and everything, after I tried so hard before I got a job. Could I really go through that again? Eventually, you know...my mental health came first. I had to try again, and again, and again."

Thankfully, there are employment opportunities that Amanda can access to help her find a company that maximizes her strengths while supporting her weaknesses.

EMPLOYMENT OPPORTUNITIES

Finding employment when you have autism can seem like an intimidating task, but it is not impossible. Many people with ASD enjoy successful— even famous—careers. As I have spoken of before, having autism does not mean that it becomes all that you are. Be sure to talk to your teen and reassure them. Let them know that they may face challenges, but they can still be gainfully employed and achieve their goals.

The struggles your teen may face with socialization makes it very important for them to become well-versed in the area they want to work in. Help your teen put together a portfolio of their work, and practice going for job interviews with them. You can also model common workplace interactions they may encounter, and how to respond. Make sure they thoroughly research any company they want to work at to learn as much about the organization as possible. When your teen goes for an interview, advise them to focus on selling their skills and to make their possible employers aware of their social limitations.

Some career paths commonly recommended for autistic people are:

- Journalism
- Librarian
- Historian
- Manufacturing
- Videography and photography
- Computer Science
- Auto Technician
- Research
- Animal Science
- Art and Design

There are also government initiatives and private organizations that offer support for people with ASD who are seeking employment.

- Vocational Rehabilitation Agencies – An agency is present in each state, and helps people with disabilities in finding and maintaining jobs. https://www.csavr.org/stateagencydirectory
- The nonPareil Institute – This non-profit organization trains adults with autism and prepares them for the higher academic and the working world. https://npusa.org/
- Exceptional Minds – This California-based company offers job training, hands-on experience, and career placement. https://exceptional-minds.org/
- PACER's National Parent Center on Transition and Employment – A center that educates parents so that they are better able to help their children through teenhood into adulthood. It offers information on disability rights, jobs, and job supports. https://www.pacer.org/transition/

- U.S. Department of Labor – This department offers employment resources, programs, and support for people with disabilities. https://www.dol.gov/
- Spectrum Careers – this site helps autistic individuals find jobs. https://jobs.spectrum.com/

Places like Microsoft and Walgreens have also implemented programs geared towards hiring people with special needs.

RESOURCES

Autism Society

Resources for Families

The Autism Society provides resources for families of individuals with autism, including teenagers. The website includes information on education, healthcare, and community support. https://autismsociety.org/

Grants and Scholarships

They also offer grants and scholarships for individuals with autism and their families. https://www.myautism.org/all-about-autism/grants-andscholarships

National Autism Association

Resources for Parents

The National Autism Association provides resources for parents of individuals with autism, including teenagers. The website includes information on advocacy, safety, and support groups. https://nationalautismassociation.org/

Helping Hand Program

This program provides financial assistance to families who are in need of medical or therapeutic interventions for their child with autism. The Helping Hand Program offers funding for services such as biomedical treatments, therapy, and special education. https://nationalautismassociation.org/

Interactive Autism Network

Parent Resources

The Interactive Autism Network provides resources for parents of individuals with autism, including teenagers. The website includes information on interventions, research, and community support. https://www.kennedykrieger.org/stories/interactive-autism-networkian

Autism Parenting Magazine

Parenting Resources

Autism Parenting Magazine provides resources for parents of individuals with autism, including teenagers. The website includes information on education, behavior management, and therapy. https://www.autismparentingmagazine.com/

Family Voices

Autism Resources

Family Voices provides resources for families of individuals with special healthcare needs, including those with autism. The website includes information on healthcare, education, and community support. https://paautism.org/support_group/philadelphia_family_voices/ http://autismresourcesinmaryland.weebly.com/family-voices.html

Financial Resources

They also provide resources for families of children with special healthcare needs, including those with autism. The website includes information on financial assistance programs, such as Medicaid and CHIP, as well as private foundations and non-profit organizations that offer funding for healthcare and education. https://www. familyvoicesofwashington.org/family-caregivers/ financial-resources/

Parent to Parent USA

State Chapters

Parent to Parent USA provides support and resources for families of children with special healthcare needs, including those with autism. The website includes information on state chapters, which offer one-on-one emotional and informational support for families. https://www.p2pusa.org/

National Parent Helpline

Autism and Special Needs Support

The National Parent Helpline offers emotional support and resources for parents of children with autism and special needs. The helpline provides a listening ear, information on resources and services, and referrals to local support groups and organizations. https://www.nationalparenthelpline.org/

It's important to note that funding and support opportunities may vary by location and individual circumstances. It may be helpful to connect with local autism organizations or support groups for additional resources and guidance.

Apps to Try Out

- **Choiceworks** - This app helps to promote independence and reduce anxiety by allowing teens to create visual schedules and make choices. https://learningworksforkids.com/apps/choiceworks/
- **Brain Parade** - This app is designed to help improve communication and social skills for teens with autism. It includes visual scenes and flashcards to help teens learn and communicate. https://www.crunchbase.com/organization/brain-parade
- **Autism Tracker Pro** - This app allows parents to track their teen's behavior, mood, and progress. It includes customizable data tracking and analysis tools. https://apps.apple.com/us/app/autism-tracker-pro/id478225574
- **Proloquo2Go** - This app is designed to help teens with autism communicate more effectively. It includes customizable voice output and vocabulary options. https://www.assistiveware.com/products/proloquo2go
- **Autism Emotion** - This app helps teens with autism identify and express emotions. It includes interactive stories and activities to teach emotion recognition and social skills. https://apps.apple.com/us/app/autism-emotion/id550027186
- **AutisMate** - This app is designed to help teens with autism develop social and communication skills. It includes customizable visual scenes and interactive stories. https://learningworksforkids.com/apps/autismate/
- **Task Analyzing Prompting** - This app helps teens with autism learn and complete tasks independently. It includes customizable task analyses and prompting tools. https://apps.apple.com/us/app/taskanalysislife/id1254481752
- **iEarnedThat** - This app is designed to help parents and teens track rewards and incentives. It includes customizable reward systems and tracking tools. https://sites.google.com/site/

musicandspecialeducation/home/ resources/related-website/
behavior-modification/iearnedthat

- **Autism Therapy with MITA** - This app is designed to help teens with autism improve cognitive and social skills through gameplay. It includes personalized training programs and progress tracking tools. https://clinicaltrials.gov/ct2/show/NCT02708290

- **Touch and Learn - Emotions** - This app helps teens with autism learn about emotions and social skills. It includes interactive games and activities to teach emotion recognition and social cues. https://apps.apple.com/us/app/touch-and-learn-emotions/ id451685022

CONCLUSION

Finally, your autism journey with your teen is unique. It will have many hills and valleys just like the journey through their beginning years. I am beginning on my journey with my teenager and have found so many wonderful people to help me along the way. I suggest you find a village, "your" community who can provide the kind of support "you" need. That can mean individuals outside of your ethnic or cultural background. Connectivity with human beings happens in many different ways. And I've found the old saying - "Not all skin folk is kin folk" can be applied when it comes to figuring out how to handle challenges with your child. When you have a village, often it gives you time to rest, re-evaluate, re-consider and restructure strategies that can make life a whole lot easier.

Autism Spectrum Disorder as you have hopefully gathered from reading this book is extremely varied. One size does not fit all. Just like the Black community, Latino community or any other community is not a monolith, neither is the ASD community. So, if your child and your experiences are different, and you don't seem to see anyone who is experiencing the same thing, don't despair. Likely you just haven't run into them yet. And when you do, be sure to seize the opportunity to connect.

I shared in this book a section about safety. This was not because I wanted to scare or disturb readers. Rather, it was an attempt to give voice to some of the issues that often Black and Brown people have shared behind closed doors but not shared in public. It's important to share these experiences publicly in effort to make change. This is so that others who have had similar experiences know they aren't alone. And It's to encourage you as a parent (whether you are BIOPIC or not) to advocate in your own community. This is so elected officials and law enforcement nationwide change policies so that they and others can feel and remain safe.

Raising your autistic child can be challenging on a number of levels, and this can get harder as they enter their teen years. My final advice is instead of taking advice and instruction from people who have no idea what autism is, spend some time discovering, exploring, and leveraging those things that make your child unique and interesting. Maximize their strengths and never look back.

REFERENCES

Antonatos, L. (2023, May 15). *How to find a great therapist for your teen.* Choosing Therapy. https://www.choosingtherapy.com/find-teen-therapist/

Anxiety: Autistic children and teenagers (n.d.). Raising Children. https://raisingchildren.net.au/autism/health-wellbeing/mental-health/anxiety-asd

ARC Autism Now (2011, March 29). *On the job.* https://autismnow.org/on-the-job/employment-research-and-reports/

Augmentative and alternative communication: Autistic children (n.d.). Raising Children. https://raisingchildren.net.au/autism/communicating-relationships/communicating/augmentative-communication-asd

Autism after high school: Nine tips to help teens transition to adulthood. (2018, September 26). UT Southwestern Medical Center. https://utswmed.org/medblog/autism-transition-teens/

Autism: early signs in young children. (2022, October 25). Raising Children. https://raisingchildren.net.au/autism/learning-about-autism/assessment-diagnosis/early-signs-of-asd

Autism myths and causes (n.d.) Autistica. https://www.autistica.org.uk/what-is-autism/autism-myths-and-causes

Autism: signs in older children and teenagers. (2022, October 26). Raising Children. https://raisingchildren.net.au/autism/learning-about-autism/assessment-diagnosis/signs-of-asd-in-teens

Autism spectrum disorder (ASD). (2023, February 9). NHS Inform. https://www.nhsinform.scot/illnesses-and-conditions/brain-nerves-and-spinal-cord/autism-spectrum-disorder-asd

Aylward, B. S., Gal-Szabo, D. E., & Taraman, S. (2021). Racial, ethnic, and sociodemographic disparities in diagnosis of children with autism spectrum disorder. *Journal of Developmental & Behavioral Pediatrics, 42*(8), 682–689. https://doi.org/10.1097/DBP.0000000000000996

Ball, E. & Jeffery-Wilensky, J. (2020, November 26). *Why autism training for police isn't enough.* Spectrum News. https://www.spectrumnews.org/news/why-autism-training-for-police-isnt-enough/

Barbera, M. (2017, June 1). *When a child with autism will not take medicine.* Dr. Mary Barbera. https://marybarbera.com/child-with-autism-not-take-medicine/

Brickman, M., & Elice, R. (2013). *The Addams family: A new musical comedy.* Theatrical Rights Worldwide. https://static1.squarespace.com/static/51c3f070e4b011cb373cb4ea/t/56a31d6005f8e2da31194f8e/1453530469899/Addams+Family+Script.pdf

Bullying: Autistic children and teenagers. (n.d.). Raising Children. https://raisingchildren.net.au/autism/behaviour/common-concerns/bullying-asd

Bush, S. (n.d.). *Sophia Bush quotes.* Brainy Quote. https://www.brainyquote.com/quotes/sophia_bush_410469

Campbell, B. (n.d.) *"How do you eat an elephant?" Chunking and chaining with task analysis.* Texas Education Agency. https://www.txautism.net/blog/how-do-you-eat-an-elephant-chunking-and-chaining-with-task-analysis

Centers for Disease Prevention and Control. (n.d.) *Signs and symptoms of autistic spectrum disorder.* https://www.cdc.gov/ncbddd/autism/signs.html

Centers for Disease Prevention and Control. (n.d.) *What is autism spectrum disorder?* https://www.cdc.gov/ncbddd/autism/facts.html

Chen, G. (2023, January 31). *5 tips to help your autistic child excel in public schools.* Public School Review. https://www.publicschoolreview.com/blog/5-tips-for-helping-your-autistic-child-excel-in-public-schools

Child sexual abuse: Keeping autistic children and teenagers safe. (2023, May 4). Raising Children. https://raisingchildren.net.au/autism/health-wellbeing/autism-child-sexual-abuse/child-sexual-abuse-keeping-autistic-children-teens-safe

Conlon, C. (2022, September 26). *Why is it important to focus on your strengths?* Life Hack. https://www.lifehack.org/articles/productivity/why-focusing-on-your-strengths-is-the-best-philosophy.html

Conversational skills for autistic pre-teens and teenagers. (n.d.). Raising Children. https://raisingchildren.net.au/autism/communicating-relationships/communicating/conversation-skills-for-teens-with-asd

Creating safety plans for people with autism. (n.d.) Autism Speaks. https://www.autismspeaks.org/creating-safety-plans-people-autism

Drake, K. (2022, March 10). *Finding fulfilling jobs if you're autistic.* PsychCentral. https://psychcentral.com/autism/jobs-for-autistic-people

Erbentraut, J. (2015, May 7). *How these 4 major companies are tackling the autism unemployment rate.* Huffpost. https://www.huffpost.com/entry/autism-employment_n_7216310

GCFGlobal (n.d.) *What is meetup?* https://edu.gcfglobal.org/en/meetup/what-is-meetup/1/#

Gibbs, V., Hudson, J., & Pellicano, E. (2022). The extent and nature of autistic people's violence experiences during adulthood: A cross-sectional study of victimisation. *Journal of Autism and Developmental Disorders*, 1-16. https://doi.org/10.1007/s10803-022-05647-3

Grandin, T. (1999, November). *Choosing the right job for people with autism or asperger's syndrome.* Indiana University Bloomington. https://www.iidc.indiana.edu/irca/articles/choosing-the-right-job-for-people-with-autism-or-aspergers-syndrome.html

Hakim, H. (2022, March 1). *Living with ASD: How can you maintain cleanliness and hygiene?* Hyper Lychee. https://hyperlychee.com/blogs/articles/living-with-asd-how-can-you-maintain-cleanliness-and-hygiene

Hanson, H. (2020, July 20). *Autistic people talk to themselves, so what? – The real talk on self-talk.* The Life Autistic. https://thelifeautistic.com/2020/07/20/when-autistic-people-talk-to-themselves-the-real-talk-on-self-talk/

Harris, C. (2020, May 5). *How to talk to your teenagers about self-care.* Courtney Harris Coaching. https://courtneyharriscoaching.com/talking-to-teenagers-about-self-care/

Hill, T. J. & Widgery, A. (2022, February 9). *Mental health emergencies, law enforcement and deflection pathways.* National Conference of State Legislatures. 10,14 https://www.ncsl.org/state-legislatures-news/details/mental-health-emergencies-law-enforcement-and-deflection-pathways

How to choose the best therapist for autism. (2019, July 11). Collaborative Therapeutic Services. https://www.therapycts.com/blog/2019/7/11/how-to-choose-the-best-therapist-for-autism

How to pursue an autism diagnosis as an adult (2022, April 14). Cleveland Clinic. https://health.clevelandclinic.org/adult-autism-diagnosis/

How to stop my child talking to himself? (n.d.) Autism Partnership. http://www.autismpartnership.com.hk/en/news/ap-connect/how-to-stop-my-child-talking-to-himself/

Hume, K. (2008). Transition time: Helping individuals on the autism spectrum move successfully from one activity to another. *The Reporter, 13*(2), 6-10. https://www.iidc.indiana.edu/irca/articles/transition-time-helping-individuals-on-the-autism-spectrum-move-successfully-from-one-activity-to-another.html

Hurley, J. (2019, August 19). *Helping children with autism get ready for the school bus.* Autism Speaks. https://www.autismspeaks.org/blog/helping-children-autism-get-ready-school-bus

Hutten, M. (n.d.). *Aspergers teens and "sex education".* My Aspergers Child. https://www.myaspergerschild.com/2010/10/aspergers-teens-and-sex-education.html

Hutten, M. (n.d.) *Self-advocacy and self-disclosure: Advice for teens on the autism spectrum.* My Aspergers Child. https://www.myaspergerschild.com/2015/09/self-advocacy-self-disclosure-advice.html

Hutten, M. (n.d.) *Thriving in adolescence and preparing for adulthood: Help for teens on the autism spectrum.* My Aspergers Child. https://www.myaspergerschild.com/2017/05/thriving-in-adolescence-and-preparing.html

Jewell, T. (2021, November 12). *What are the signs of autism in teenagers?* Healthline. https://www.healthline.com/health/autism-in-teens

Koegel, L.K., & LaZebnik, C.S. (2010) *Growing up on the spectrum: A guide to life, love, and learning for teens and young adults with autism and asperger's.* Penguin Books.

Laber-Warren, E. (2021, May 12). *The benefits of special interests in autism.* Spectrum News. https://www.spectrumnews.org/features/deep-dive/the-benefits-of-special-interests-in-autism/

Lamoreux, K. (2021, June 29). *Medications for autism spectrum disorder.* Psych Central. https://psychcentral.com/autism/medications-for-autism

Lang, A. (2015, September 9). *How to talk to kids on the spectrum about sex.* Birds and Bees Kids. https://birdsandbeesandkids.com/autism-spectrum-sex-talk/

Lawson, C. (1992, October 8). *At home with: Marian Wright Edelman; a sense of place called family.* The New York Times. https://www.nytimes.com/1992/10/08/garden/at-home-with-marian-wright-edelman-a-sense-of-place-called-family.html

Laxman, D. J., Taylor, J. L., DaWalt, L. S., Greenberg, J. S., & Mailick, M. R. (2019). Loss in services precedes high school exit for teens with autism spectrum disorder: A longitudinal study. *Autism Research, 12*(6), 911–921. https://doi.org/10.1002/aur.2113

Lovering, N. (2022, November 10). *Autism and savant syndrome: What to know.* PsychCentral. https://psychcentral.com/autism/savant-autism

McNair, J. (2021, August 25). *How to avoid overidentifying black male students for special education.* Edutopia. https://www.edutopia.org/article/how-avoid-overidentifying-black-male-students-special-education/

Meltdowns: Autistic children and teenagers. (2022, April 28). Raising Children. https://raisingchildren.net.au/autism/behaviour/common-concerns/meltdowns-autistic-children-teenagers

Miller-Merrell, J. (2016, April 12). *27 companies who hire adults with autism.* Workology. https://workology.com/companies-hiring-adults-with-autism/

National Autistic Society. (2020, August 14). *Meltdown- a guide for all audiences.* National Autistic Society. https://www.autism.org.uk/advice-and-guidance/topics/behaviour/meltdowns/all-audiences

National Autistic Society (n.d.) *Anxiety.* https://www.autism.org.uk/advice-and-guidance/topics/mental-health/anxiety

Nightengale, L. (2021, December 21). *The autism spectrum explained*. OSF Healthcare. https://www.osfhealthcare.org/blog/the-autism-spectrum-explained/

Novick, B. (2021, October 9). *Dating advice for teens on the spectrum*. Autism Parenting Magazine. https://www.autismparentingmagazine.com/dating-advice-for-teens/

Office for Victims of Crime (n.d.) *Victims with disabilities*. https://ovc.ojp.gov/topics/victims-with-disabilities

Omahen, E. (2022, February 22). *Easy ways to help your child with self-regulation*. Autism Parenting Magazine. https://www.autismparentingmagazine.com/easy-ways-with-self-regulation/

One Central Health (2020, October 30). *10 myths about autism spectrum disorder*. https://www.onecentralhealth.com.au/autism/10-myths-about-autism/

Paying attention: autistic children and teenagers (n.d.). Raising Children. https://raisingchildren.net.au/autism/communicating-relationships/communicating/paying-attention-asd

Pearson, J. N. & Meadan, H. (2018). African American parents' perceptions of diagnosis and services for children with autism. *Education and Training in Autism and Developmental Disabilities, 53*(1), 17-32. https://files.eric.ed.gov/fulltext/EJ1179135.pdf

Perry, D. M., & Carter-Long, L. (2016). *The Ruderman white paper on media coverage of law enforcement use of force and disability*. Ruderman Family Foundation. 5,7 https://rudermanfoundation.org/wp-content/uploads/2017/08/MediaStudy-PoliceDisability_final-final.pdf

Personal hygiene and autistic teenagers (2021, January 22). Raising Children. https://raisingchildren.net.au/autism/health-wellbeing/toileting-hygiene/personal-hygiene-autistic-teens

Platzman-Weinstock, C. (2019, July 17). *The deep emotional ties between depression and autism.* Spectrum News. https://www.spectrumnews.org/features/deep-dive/the-deep-emotional-ties-between-depression-and-autism/

Positive reinforcement autism. (2022, June 2). Golden Care Therapy. https://www.goldencaretherapy.com/positive-reinforcement-autism

Romantic relationships and feelings: autistic teenagers. (2020, September 12). Raising Children. https://raisingchildren.net.au/autism/development/sexual-development/romantic-relationships-feelings-autistic-teenagers

Rutgers University (n.d.) *LaChan Hannon.* https://sasn.rutgers.edu/about-us/faculty-staff/lachan-hannon

Sarris, M. (2013, July 23). *Autism in the teen years: What to expect, how to help.* Kennedy Krieger Institute. https://www.kennedykrieger.org/stories/interactive-autism-network-ian/autism_in_teens

Sarris, M. (2020, October 29). *Understanding aggressive behavior in autism.* Discover Spark. https://sparkforautism.org/discover_article/understanding-aggressive-behavior-in-autism/

Schlikerman, B. & Ford, L. (2012, February 2). *Teen with autism shot to death by police.* The Chicago Tribune. https://www.chicagotribune.com/news/ct-xpm-2012-02-02-ct-met-calumet-city-shooting-20120202-story.html

Schweitzer, A. (2017), *Reverence for life: The words of Albert Schweitzer.* Amazon.

Seelig, C. (1952) *Ideas and opinions by Albert Einstein.* Wings Books.

Sensory issues. (n.d.) Autism Speaks. https://www.autismspeaks.org/sensory-issues

Sensory issues in teens with autism spectrum disorder. (n.d.) Discover Seven Stars. https://discoversevenstars.com/about-us/who-we-help/sensory-issues/

Sexuality instruction for tweens, teens, and young adults. (2020, June 3). Children's Hospital of Philadelphia Research Institute. https://www. research.chop.edu/car-autism-roadmap/sexuality-instruction-for-tweens-teens-and-young-adults

Shattuck, P. T., Rast, J., Roux, A. M., Anderson, K. A., Benevides, T., Garfield, T., McGhee-Hassrick, E., & Kuo, A. (2019). *National autism indicators report: High school students on the autism spectrum.* The Policy Impact Project. https:// policyimpactproject.org/high-school-students-on-the-autism-spectrum/

Silvertant, M. (2021, May 4). *The autistic experience of overwhelm.* Embrace Autism. https://embrace-autism.com/the-autistic-experience-of-overwhelm/

SingleCare Team (2021, September 15). *Sensory overload: Teaching children with autism to take medication.* Single Care. https://www. singlecare.com/blog/teaching-children-with-autism-medication/

Six most common causes of anger in relation to autism disorders. (2013, May 22). Pasadena Villa. https://www.pasadenavilla.com/resources/blog/common-causes-of-anger-autism/

Social skills and autism. (n.d.) Autism Speaks. https://www.autismspeaks. org/social-skills-and-autism

Social skills classes produce lasting benefits for adults with autism. (2018, August 25). Autism Speaks. https://www.autismspeaks.org/news/social-skills-classes-produce-lasting-benefits-adults-autism

Stigler, K. (n.d.) *When should a parent consider medication for their child with autism spectrum disorder?* American Academy of Child and Adolescent Psychiatry. https://www.aacap.org/AACAP/Families_and_Youth/Resource_Centers/Autism_Resource_Center/When_Should_a_Parent_Consider_Medication_for_their_Child_with_an_Autism_Spectrum_Disorder.aspx

Stimming: Autistic children and teenagers. (2022, August 25). Raising Children. https://raisingchildren.net.au/autism/behaviour/common-concerns/stimming-asd

Tamara. (2022, May 30). *10 ways to make transitions easier for your autistic child*. Autism and ADHD Connection. https://autismadhdconnection.com/10-ways-to-make-transitions-easier-for-your-autistic-child/

Toileting. (n.d.) Center for Autism Middletown. http://teenage-resource.middletownautism.com/teenage-issues-and-strategies/life-skills/self-care/toileting/

Uljarević, M., Alvares, G. A., Steele, M., Edwards, J., Frazier, T. W., Hardan, A. Y., & Whitehouse, A. J. (2022). Toward better characterization of restricted and unusual interests in youth with autism. *Autism, 26*(5), 1296–1304. https://doi.org/10.1177/13623613211056720

U.S. Department of Health and Human Services (n.d.). *Employment.* https://iacc.hhs.gov/resources/employment/websites/

VanBergeijk, E. (2009, April 1). *Travel training for higher functioning individuals on the autism spectrum.* Autism Spectrum News. https://autismspectrumnews.org/travel-training-for-higher-functioning-individuals-on-the-autism-spectrum/

Westendorf-Coelho, S. L. (2011). *The world according to August - one good friend.* Goodreads. https://www.goodreads.com/work/quotes/17499553-the-world-according-to-august—one-good-friend

Zeliadt, N. (2018, January 17). *Sensory sensitivity may share genetic roots with autism.* Spectrum News. https://www.spectrumnews.org/news/sensory-sensitivity-may-share-genetic-roots-autism/

Printed in the United States
by Baker & Taylor Publisher Services